SALES AUTOPSY

50 Postmortems Reveal
What Killed the Sale
(and What Might Have Saved It)

DAN SEIDMAN

KAPLAN PUBLISHING

This publication is designed to provide accurate and authoritative information in regard to the subject matter covered. It is sold with the understanding that the publisher is not engaged in rendering legal, accounting, or other professional service. If legal advice or other expert assistance is required, the services of a competent professional should be sought.

President, Kaplan Publishing: Roy Lipner
Vice President and Publisher: Maureen McMahon
Acquisitions Editor: Karen Murphy
Development Editor: Trey Thoelcke
Production Editor: Leah Strauss
Typesetter: Caitlin Ostrow
Cover Designer: Design Solutions

Published by Kaplan Publishing, a division of Kaplan, Inc.

Printed in the United States of America

06 07 08 10 9 8 7 6 5 4 3 2 1

Library of Congress Cataloging-in-Publication Data

Seidman, Dan.
  Sales autopsy / Dan Seidman.
    p. cm.
  ISBN-13: 978-1-4195-4055-4
  ISBN-10: 1-4195-4055-6
  1. Selling. I. Title.
  HF5438.25.S4357 2006
  658.85--dc22

                                    2006020383

Kaplan Publishing books are available at special quantity discounts to use for sales promotions, employee premiums, or educational purposes. Please call our Special Sales Department to order or for more information at 800-621-9621, ext. 4444, e-mail kaplanpubsales@kaplan.com, or write to Kaplan Publishing, 30 South Wacker Drive, Suite 2500, Chicago, IL 60606-7481.

Contents

Introduction

It was a dreadful day's end for Mark. His best customer called, out of courtesy, to say he was switching vendors. There went 25 percent of his revenue. Then another major prospect phoned about 5:15 PM (hoping he'd get Mark's voice mail) to say he was going with someone else. The future was fizzling fast for this good friend sitting next to me.

And Mark wasn't just a friend because his wife packed extra sushi in his lunch to share with me. He was a smart sales pro, a plodder who just kept working the phones whether times were good or wretched. His day was now ending with pats on the back and condolences. You'd have thought we were at a funeral.

I came to work early the next day, 5:30 to be exact—the time when I normally pulled practical jokes on my peers. (I'd never been caught; my college days were paying off in the workplace.) I knelt down next to Mark's desk, dug out my big white piece of sidewalk chalk, and began to draw an outline of a body.

I was gone long before anyone arrived but coincidently met Mark in the parking lot as we both came to work—me for the second time. People were already gathering around Mark's desk and laughing when we came in. They didn't know it then, but they were there for the birth of my Sales Autopsy logo.

While sales disasters (other people's, of course) often provide needed humor, they can also provide much more. First, laughter is refreshing. It has a healing effect on the soul and body. This is why I collect sales horror stories. We're in a tough business and could use some relief. In fact, when I speak, my audiences would rather hear their peers' sales blunders during the "confession session" than absorb selling wisdom or strategies from the rest of my program.

Next, and most important, your ability to recover quickly from irritating, even disastrous, experiences in your sales life is a measure of your mental health. You must move forward quickly, perhaps taking time to learn a quick lesson from the experience, in order to keep focused on your goal to build your business.

Have you ever had the crushing feeling that there's somehow a gap between you and greatness? Throughout this book you will discover, through laughter and the hard-earned experience of those who've gone before you, ways to close that gap.

The ideas, strategies, and concepts inside these pages have been compiled from more than 600 sales horror stories

and ensuing interviews with your peers. Through these stories and my training and coaching practice, I've discovered
three larger commonalities among world-class sales professionals. They all

1. qualify and disqualify prospects quickly;

2. move beyond traditional 20th century selling
   techniques and employ newer strategies that
   savvy prospects can't counter; and

3. invest in themselves in three ways: by upgrading
   appearance, utilizing great tools, and boosting
   their selling brainpower.

How can you quickly attain *elite* status in selling? Share
what you discover here with someone else who sells. When
you become the teacher, you learn most quickly. And the
faster you put your most useful learning moments from this
book into play, the more quickly you become the master.

My hope is that you are not just affected but *inspired
to improve* from the ideas you're about to absorb. I trust
this book becomes a blessing to your income, career, and,
mostly, your family.

Dan Seidman, SalesAutopsy.com
Barrington, IL

P.S. Did you know that if you lay all the really bad
prospects from end to end around the world, 76 percent
of them would drown?

CHAPTER ONE

Thank God That Didn't Happen to Me!

My Top Five Sales Horror Stories

How to get started? Well, let's begin with some of the most dramatic experiences from my collection of selling blunders. This was a tough call to make. How'd you like to plow through 600 sales tales, looking for the best of the worst?

More than just amazing encounters that provide some laughs at the expense of our sales colleagues who've crashed and burned before us, these horror stories also each come with a brief postmortem or lesson learned—to show what (if anything) could be learned from the experience and what just might have turned the moment around.

We've all been there, and I trust you'll want to share these stories with your sales colleagues. You know they could use a lift after a rough day with tough prospects.

#5 Buyer with Big Ears Ends a Sale

In Tom's rookie days as a life insurance salesperson with a large firm, he had to be accompanied by his boss on all sales calls.

Tom's very first client meeting with his manager was with a successful female attorney. Tom watched as his boss smoothly convinced this prospect of her need for not only personal coverage but buy/sell policies for the law firm as well. Before leaving, Tom's manager asked the female attorney for some referrals and was rewarded with several highly qualified names.

As they waited for the elevator, the two agents didn't realize how well sound carried in the historic, marble office building. Tom's manager turned to his new protégé and said, "You see, Tommy, this business is so easy, it's like shootin' fish in a barrel."

Moments later the words "I heard that" echoed down the hall.

"Get back here!" She barked.

Tom and his manager walked into a cold room to a very heated client. The angry attorney waved their literature at them and asked for her life insurance applications and the list of referrals.

She slowly tore everything in half, then tore it again and dramatically walked to the shredder and fed their paperwork into the machine.

To this day, Tom still has a serious aversion to asking for referrals. He remains deathly afraid to use this strategy, even after a successful sale, despite it being the easiest way to gather new business.

> **Postmortem:** What a plot: Drama with great dialogue on a sales call! And revenge to top it off! Just when you thought it was safe, new clients are reversing course and killing sales. There are lots of lessons here. Let's focus on one—and it's not asking for referrals. (How many more times are we going to have the phrase "ask for referrals" pounded into us?) This lesson is about handling adversity. How well do you maintain your professional demeanor, even when the weather turns nasty? You'll see this addressed in detail later in the book.

● ● ●

#4 Baaad Luck at the Farm

It suddenly didn't even matter that this financial services rep had to spend another $5 to wash his dust-covered car after leaving this prospect's property.

John and his partner had finished a tough series of sales calls on a large corporate farm. The owner was taking on a complete insurance package—their company was covering everything. The men were looking at almost $50,000 staring them in the, well, bank accounts.

It didn't even matter that he had to thoroughly scrape the bottom of his shoes before soiling the carpet of his car again. A Chicago city boy like John could make good money in the country—even with minimal selling skills and zero knowledge about the farming life.

So there sat the four of them, the owner with hands folded on his desk and his accountant with hands folded atop a large leather book—the company checkbook. John and his partner beamed at each other and pulled out one last form.

"In order for us to see that you're completely covered, we need your livestock totals." John began to call out the animal names and receive the numbers of each herd, with babies listed separately—beef cattle, milk cows, horses, and pigs, then . . .

"Sheep?" 120 was the reply.

"E-wees?"

"Huh?" grunted the owner.

"E-wees." John said, clearly mispronouncing the word again. "How many e-wees you got?"

"Let me see that form," the farmer said.

John pointed and the farmer yelled, "That's ewes, you idiot! Have you ever been on a farm? How are you supposed to help me with my business if you know nothing about farming? You know what? Don't even answer that, just get out, get out of my office!"

They walked quickly to the car, not even stopping to clean their shoes, hopped in, and drove away, $50,000 poorer.

Postmortem: John will be counting sheep, instead of money, in his sleep tonight. Okay, so John was a bit short in his product knowledge training, but let's focus on another not-so-obvious lesson. What do you do when you blow it on a call? Do you collapse and write it off? One suggestion I offer in situations like this is to be very, very remorseful. Apologize for your mistake, then say something like, "Oh Lord. You must think I'm my company's village idiot. I'm so sorry. If you don't want to do business with me, I completely understand." Don't be surprised if the prospect says, "Hey, that's okay. I've done some dumb things, too. Let's keep going." If you feel bad, you'll make most people want to help you to not be so hard on yourself—and you could save a sale.

● ● ●

#3 Cold Wind, Cops, and a Car

Welcome to winter, John thought as he stood inside the Quebec airport terminal. Outside the snow was sideways from a furious wind.

John and his partner had flown in for a sales call—from the sunny south—Alabama, USA. The French gal at the Hertz counter pegged them immediately and began speaking in beautifully accented English.

John gestured over his shoulder to the weather. "Do we have to walk to the shuttle, walk to the Hertz lot, then walk outside again to our car?"

She smiled and shook her head. "Sir, we will deliver your auto right outside that door. It's a blue Ford Crown Victoria."

Five minutes later, a big blue Ford pulled up and a man jumped out and ran into the terminal. The two men looked at him and the guy nodded as he walked by. John glanced at his partner, who said "Let's go!", and they dashed into the snow.

Thank goodness the car was running and warm. They drove out of the airport and John told his colleague to pull the map out of the glove compartment where the car rental agent had said it awaited them.

When the door was popped open, paper trash and other garbage spilled onto his lap.

"This car is a dump!" John couldn't believe Hertz would give them a vehicle without cleaning it first. And then that little light went off overhead. They looked at each other and said together, "It's not our car."

A glance into the rearview mirror and the men realized that someone else had come to the same conclusion. Another light was going off, a flashing light from a Royal Canadian Mounted Police (RCMP) vehicle.

Well, of course, they had taken that poor guy's car who nodded to them, thinking he was giving the "go ahead and get in" signal, when really, he was just rushing in from the cold.

The RCMP were very professional throughout, doing their best to suppress their grins at the stupid mistake. And Hertz apologized for the confusion, telling the two of them that they wouldn't be charged for driving the car that Hertz intended they use—once they finally got it.

John said his lesson was that impatience can have lots of unexpected consequences.

Postmortem: John, a wanted man north of the border! He's right, though. Life is getting too fast. We're always in a hurry. We cram cell phone conversations into our downtime during the day. We can't even relax and enjoy television commercials anymore. Our clients and prospects want us to get quickly to the point as well. We rush to sell and this is when mistakes happen. BUT, if you learn to slow down and calm down, it will increase your energy when you need it most. Be wise about managing your time; take time for yourself. You body, your mind, and, most important, your family will love you for those times you choose to slow down.

● ● ●

#2 Three-Ring-Circus Selling

It was a hot August day, and Scott and his colleague were about 45 minutes early to demonstrate their data technology services. To kill the time, they decided to get a cold drink at the closest convenience store. Scott bought a superlarge frozen cherry drink, and his partner got a lime-flavored one.

They drove back to the prospect's building and sat in the visitor's spot, mentally preparing while they finished their frozen drinks. When they were ready to go, Scott looked over and saw his partner's mouth, lips, teeth, and tongue were bright green—really bright, like a clown's. He grabbed the rearview mirror and flipped it toward his face, whose features were now glowing red.

The dramatic colors seemed indelible and even an oily rag under the car seat was useless for obvious reasons. But it was time for their appointment, so the two guys walked to the entrance. People in the lobby actually burst out laughing at the sight of these two sales bozos. They sat down with the president but were so rattled about how silly they looked that they gave the most uninspiring presentation of their careers. They were not asked back.

Postmortem: Obviously, thinking more carefully about your actions just before a sales call is important. However, the psychological reason a call like this fails is that you can't gain rapport with a prospect who is uncomfortable being pitched by circus clowns. It might work if you happen to be calling on another circus clown or the ringmaster or, minimally, the guy with the shovel who follows behind the elephant. There's no hope for a rep who makes an unprofessional first impression on a prospect. I told this tale while speaking to the worldwide conference of the Sales & Marketing Executives International and received a smart suggestion for Scott: Bring frozen drinks for the prospect—it might just save the sale.

● ● ●

And my personal #1, SalesAutopsy.com fan's favorite and most requested sales horror story of all time . . .

#1 Foot in Mouth Kills Salesman

Rick sells printing services, and he's probably not as good as he is persistent. It took six months of phone calls and mailed literature to finally get into the president's office of a company that the rep wanted to sell very badly. It took less than 30 seconds to undo half a year of time and effort.

Rick had finally nailed this guy down to an appointment and wanted to make a very good first impression. He figured that this president would look at him as either a strong salesman or a pest. He would dispose of a pest as quickly as he could, so as Rick walked into the executive's office, he looked for something on the wall or on his desk to use for a little opening small talk.

There it was! "John Madden!" he cried, pointing at an 8×10 photograph on the prospect's credenza. Every sports fan knows the 300-plus-pound commentator. He's probably the best announcer around, despite a face that could stop a bus. "That's a fantastic photo! How did you get a picture of yourself with your arm around John Madden?"

Rick's rapport-building efforts crashed in flames as the shocked company president slowly answered, "That's not John Madden; that's . . . my . . . wife."

Postmortem: Our poor salesman, Rick, used an approach that was popular early in the evolution of selling. Are you like this at the initial contact with a prospect? Do you look for that fish on the wall, trophy on the shelf, or picture on the desk? We're often taught to comment on these items to break the ice. Can you distinguish yourself by being so ordinary?

Don't sound like everyone else who sells. This small talk is wasteful and disrespectful of a buyer's time. Here's a suggestion for that initial contact that many top-performing sales pros use today: Recognize that your prospects don't have the time to chat like they used to. Simply respect the prospect's time, and review what you agreed upon when you got the appointment.

Rick should have said, "Mr. Prospect, I want to respect your commitment to the time we have. When we talked on the phone you said we'd have 45 minutes to talk. Is that right? Good. What is the most serious reason you felt it was important to invite me in today?" As a sales pro, you've now honored someone's busy schedule and gotten right to business. Best of all, the prospect is about to do most of the talking.

CHAPTER TWO

Dairy Queen

Disqualify Prospects Quickly

This is the #1 problem salespeople face (yes, that would be you):

You don't disqualify your prospects quickly enough.

This holds true for just about everyone who sells, and this is right where Dairy Queen (or DQ) comes into play. This slang term for "disqualify" is not a dirty word. It's the path to a clean sales life, unless you ignore it, as our reps do throughout this chapter.

Excavating Clients

First thing in the morning and Mark had a last-minute pitch to make. The president of his Chicago ad agency heard that a Milwaukee-based crane association was reviewing their programs, and he ordered Mark to call and ask for an appointment that day—before the company finalized any decisions. Mark called and practically begged for the meeting. He then drove the two hours up I-94, completely confident that they still had a great shot at landing the business. Here's why.

Mark's agency handled loads of construction companies. In his briefcase were custom flyers and tons of testimonials with impressive pictures of earthmoving equipment. Cruise control set at 70, he smiled as he passed from Illinois into Wisconsin. There must have been six or eight crane rental companies along the highway. If you believed in omens, you'd have felt pretty good about this sales call.

He pulled up to the front door to discover the association logo was a crane, the bird with a long neck. Cool idea. Some organizations really market themselves well.

The reception area was quiet and beautifully decorated. The walls were covered not with machinery but with more cranes, hundreds and hundreds of them. It soon struck him that this association was for the preservation of, well, birds.

Mark met the decision maker and, hoping against hope, still attempted to present his company's offerings, all the while really burning with anger at his firm's and his boss's stupid misunderstanding. The executive director sat through the most uninspired sales conversation, and Mark just wished it would end.

He left the association empty-handed and embarrassed, and then had the special pleasure of being the butt of office jokes for several months. Now, even if he's in a hurry, Mark does homework on all potential clients.

Postmortem: Mark's mistake is pretty funny and presents an outstanding lesson: Do your homework on potential clients, which will help you to qualify or disqualify them. You can then focus more tightly on your exact target market.

● ● ●

In this next internationally flavored story, a sales pitch is improperly laid on the exact wrong audience . . .

Not-so-Sweet Smell of Success

Claudine sold very expensive perfumes and personal care products for one of the top international brands. And she was lucky enough to be good enough to land a job in Paris.

It was a wild existence—new culture, classy friends, fabulous clothes.

And then there was that product launch.

The company was doing a worldwide introduction of its new tanning and bronzing creams.

As a key employee, she was handed tickets to Tokyo, where a meeting was set up with that country's top 30 buyers.

Claudine nervously stood before a room full of high-powered people from the industry—all women. Her own olive skin was their first introduction to the product.

She waved the company's wares over her head and excitedly shared how their customers would look more successful, more healthy by simply applying these new products to their skin.

Their faces were a sea of blank, shocked looks.

Claudine was confused. Thinking, perhaps they didn't understand English, she switched to French. (It was a dumb thing to do, but it was the only other language she spoke.)

She was immediately interrupted by the organizer of the meeting.

"Claudine, can you show us which products you have that can make our skin whiter?"

Big blunder! In Japan's culture, common fieldworkers had darkened skin. Traditional women of status were as white as possible.

You can probably guess how many initial orders the company got from the group.

___**Postmortem:** There have been some fascinating studies done on marketing blunders. Most of them are simply a poor job of matching product and prospect. Classic tales include baby pictures on food jars in a culture that doesn't read. The picture normally shows what is contained inside (think about that). Other problems are related to colors, translation trouble, and more. The problem with international blunders is that your mistakes actually help your target market disqualify you—an interesting paradox in the sales and marketing arena. In this instance, obviously Japan is not the customer for this product. For some fascinating reading on the subject, check out David Ricks's book, *Blunders in International Business* (Blackwell Publishing, 2006).

●　●　●

In the next sales tale, a rep ignores one of his decision-making criteria for DQing his prospects and ends up with a surprise ending to his story.

Say Hello to Handcuffs

Doug, a financial services professional, made a house call to a senior citizen who responded to one of the company's direct-mail campaigns for a complimentary review of her financial situation. She was a widow, so

Doug suggested that she have one of her sons present. She did not like that idea. He then suggested her pastor, so she could have a care-giver with her. She refused that as well. But as he felt a good rapport with her, Doug decided to make an exception to his own rule against meeting with a senior alone and began his presentation in her living room. The meeting went well, and Doug returned to his office to research some choices for this well-to-do prospect.

On the second visit, she had coffee and cake waiting! She even asked him to look at a bad electrical fixture. These are good signs when you know the value of rapport. He scheduled the third and, hopefully, final meeting.

Doug put hours of groundwork into his client's situation, even contacting the Veterans Administration trying to help her with trust documents. The lawyer who sets up living trusts for Doug's clients had already done her review for free.

When he returned to her home a few days later to finalize the deal, Doug was greeted by a special police unit for organized crime!

It turned out she had Alzheimer's and had forgotten she had contacted his company. All she could remember was that a guy asking about her money was coming over. Apparently, she had been conned somewhere in her past by some guy from New York who sold her husband a bad investment, so she was angry and paranoid (a tough combination). The police were sure they were about to nail a big con artist.

John pulled out his appointment book, corporate literature, and proof that he was a legitimate, licensed financial services professional.

After verifying that the rep was for real, the police gave him a "clean bill of health" to conduct business with her. One of the officers explained to this senior that everything was okay and she could meet with him. Doug, in his anger and embarrassment, refused, since she had not followed his earlier requests to have someone present with her.

The salesman's emotions went from shock to frustration to anger. Having been through the Certified Senior Advisor program, he understood that one symptom of Alzheimer's is paranoia. Irritated that he had invested so much time in helping her investment situation, combined with a few moments of fear that the police had been ready to cart him off the jail, helped him say no to working with this woman.

Doug learned that, in the future, he should follow his system. He should stick to his belief that one should refuse to meet with single seniors unless a child, relative, or trusted friend is also with that client.

Postmortem: Doug broke one of his qualifying rules—a senior citizen should have someone he or she trusts present. Again, if you do business with people who can provide both money and headaches, you better be prepared to deal with bigger aspirin bills, troublesome clients, even defense attorneys. Bad customers can imprison us with aggravation and their need for extra attention. Decide exactly who you want to work with, and stick to your decision. You'll be glad you set standards that help you select your ideal client.

● ● ●

Rookie mistakes are common in DQing prospects. But few stories were as bizarre as this one . . .

Baby Rep Meets Prospects with Baby

First solo sales call of his life. Ryan was selling (well, trying to sell) life insurance. But because he's so excited and nervous he honestly is not sure that he even cares about making the sale. He's just thrilled to actually get an appointment.

Did you ever get a bad feeling when you walked into a prospect's place? Upon arriving at this appointment Ryan immediately felt as though he was in the wrong room. It was the dirtiest apartment the rep had ever seen. As he began to speak to the couple about life insurance— asking some basic questions—he found out the husband had "just had heart surgery last month . . . and wasn't expected to live long." So, not a good prospect.

Wow, this couple was only in their 20s. Who would ever thought this condition would exist here? After explaining there was nothing he could do for him, Ryan decided to find a way to salvage the appointment. The rookie didn't want to upset his manager when he returned to work.

So he started to work on the wife, and she agreed to take a policy! Hey, he was going to make the sale! Now this rep is fired up. As they began to fill out the health questionnaire, the woman mentions that she is pregnant. Rick was honestly stumped. He didn't know what the insurance company would do. They never talked specifically about this in training. Was this a preexisting condition? Probably, but our man was going to get this application completed if it killed him.

Once all the forms were filled out, it was time to ask for a check. But first he congratulates her on her pregnancy. The couple looks at one another and the dad says, "Please do not congratulate us. We are giving the baby up for adoption."

How many surprises is a guy going to get on one call? Ryan smiled and said, "Well, I understand it is really hard, and expensive, to raise a child these days."

Mom replies, "Yeah, and we are going to make a lot of money from THIS ONE!"

Huh? "What do you mean?"

She continues, "We got pregnant with the intention of selling our baby. A family is paying all of our expenses right now and giving us $60,000 for this kid! In fact, we may want to talk to you about investing some of this money."

Ryan could not believe what he'd heard. He described the scenario "like I'm on freaking *Jerry Springer*! This is the *Jerry Springer Show!*" The rep was so sick about what he'd heard that he decided to shake their hands and leave. He never spoke to them again. Ryan did not take any money and threw the application away.

The baby rep learned a huge lesson from his first appointment: QUALIFY the prospects!

Postmortem: Ryan is growing up fast in selling. He realized that this step in the sales process is the source of more sales frustration than any problem you can find. The reason? You head down the sales path with a bad prospect and you lose time, momentum, and money—which you can never retrieve. Again, decide today what makes a perfect prospect. This is a great exercise with a sales team or a networking group. Decide also what makes an imperfect prospect. Qualify and disqualify everybody—quickly—and you'll improve your closing ratio—guaranteed!

● ● ●

If you are in management or are an entrepreneur, you could learn from this next story that the qualifying/disqualifying dilemma also applies to hiring practices. This sales nightmare was as costly as a mistake could be . . .

Entrepreneur Meets His Dream Sales Manager

Steve was a successful telecommunications entrepreneur who met Mark at a resort. They got along fabulously. Mark was a dynamic, entertaining salesman who could carry a conversation on any topic. The two of them played golf. They went boating. They ate meals together. They were as inseparable as old college buddies.

At the end of a week of hanging out, Steve offered his newfound friend a national sales manager job. He knew nothing about Mark. But Steve felt Mark was so sharp he could handle both his company's salesforce and his clients. Mark received a company credit card, keys to the office, and an expense account.

Mark and Steve were working on a very large corporate prospect when they found themselves sitting in the boardroom of a major corporation. Seven weeks of hard work—proposals, meetings, and phone calls—were about to pay off in big numbers.

The door to the boardroom swung open, and a man in a suit pushed pass the secretary.

"Are you Mark ___?" the stranger asked.

"Sure, what's your name?" replied Steve's national sales manager.

The guy in the suit grabbed Mark's sleeve and jerked him out of the leather chair. He slammed him facedown on the boardroom table. He twisted Mark's right arm around his back. He helped Mark's right arm meet his left and joined them with stainless steel handcuffs.

In law enforcement lingo, Mark was "cuffed and stuffed."

The national sales manager was wanted on an outstanding drug warrant. There were other criminal activity warrants on his head, including physical abuse of a wife and a girlfriend and $27,000 in missing child support.

Steve's company did not land the telecommunications business of that large client. In fact, when word of what happened hit the local community, business began to dry up as contracts didn't close and existing clients fled. Steve's decision to hire his vacation buddy put the entrepreneur out of business within a year.

Postmortem: Qualifying and disqualifying are equally important inside a company. This outstanding story should have managers and entrepreneurs running to talk to companies that screen and assess employees, specifically salespeople. Steve paid for his hiring stupidity with his baby—his business that was meant to feed his family. Those horrible moments in that boardroom amounted to the most traumatic business experience of his life. Instant ulcer! Get help to identify the perfect fit as a hire for your company. This will save you tons of time interviewing the wrong candidates. It'll save the agony of training the wrong people. It'll save the duplicated effort of interviewing and hiring—again and again—once bad hires leave or are fired. Follow proven hiring procedures for all employees—top of the ladder on down. Qualify the best, and disqualify the rest. You'll be glad you learned this lesson from someone else's mistake.

●　●　●

There is a reason we discuss disqualifying prospects this early in the book. In fact, I remember exactly where I was when the truth and value of this concept hit me.

My VP of sales (in a previous selling life) asked me if I was going to bring the FBI on as a client. Absolutely! I'd told him. I was mirroring the enthusiasm the FBI buyers had shown toward me and my product. So I lay awake at night for months, dreaming of landing this prestigious government organization. In all my sales stupidity, I could not see the sign. In fact, it was years before I could translate the words in front of me. The sign said, "Buddy, you're clueless about buyers. You slobber all over them and they nod knowingly as they walk you to the door. If you'd just shut up a bit and pepper your dream appointment with some smart questions, you'd know whether your dreams are foretelling the future or just wishful thinking." It was a very large sign.

A friend of mine consoled me on this, saying that I was lucky to be in selling where I could make a wrong call about future business. In biblical times, a prophet who made one wrong prediction was not just shunned or stripped of his title, he was executed. Maybe if that noose was dangled over our heads, we'd be better at selling. I'll hang it overhead right here and now:

- Don't get better and you don't make money.

- Don't make money and you're fired.

- If you're an entrepreneur, your company moves from endangered to extinct.

From my sales stupidity, my embarrassingly inaccurate prediction, came wisdom. That wisdom is this: *You must disqualify prospects as early in the sales process as possible. By doing so, you qualify the rest as deserving your attention and energy.*

What criteria do we use to disqualify prospects?

That depends on the standards your company has set for identifying the ideal customer.

Some of those criteria might be . . .

- Do they have the money to spend?

- Is there some urgency to solve the problem you address?

- Will they give you the time to have a serious conversation about helping them?

- Are you dealing directly with the actual decision maker?

- When will the decision be made?

- Can you work on an ongoing basis with this person or company?

Here are three steps to disqualifying bad prospects:

1. Sit down one day and determine the perfect customer profile.

2. Write a list of questions to ask in order to find if they fit.

3. Relentlessly turn your back on those who don't fit.

It is that simple. Great salespeople spend more time with better prospects and less with bad ones.

I recently designed a sales training program for a financial services company. We modeled their top rep, Steve, in order to set some standards for qualifying and disqualifying potential clients. The data we had showed that the average rep wasted 12.7 hours on bad prospects. The #1 performer spent an average of 37 minutes before saying good-bye to these time wasters! The difference in closing ratios was equally dramatic. Rep average was 17.5 percent, while the top rep closed more than 76 percent of his qualified prospects. Steve was serious about dishing out Dairy Queen. His numbers speak volumes— of commission.

These are some serious numbers that might help tip you toward setting some standards in order to disqualify quickly.

Dairy Queen those low-income, poor percentage prospects. Your ability to disqualify first and fast will keep you in front of buyers who are ready, willing, and able to pay you for your products and services.

There is one more thing. There is what I call the mother of all disqualifying problems . . .

The 800-Pound Lie of Guerrilla Marketing

The biggest reason we don't do the qualifying thing well comes from a 30-year-old idea called Guerrilla

Marketing, which is based on the belief that we can use dozens of strategies to land loads of prospects. Unfortunately, there is a price to pay for these "free" lead-generation strategies.

First, let me make it clear that I love the creator of the Guerrilla Marketing concept, Jay Conrad Levinson. I've been a worshipper of Jay's thinking from the beginning of his rise to power as an author and trainer of entrepreneurial America. His books are published worldwide, and he is in constant demand as a speaker. His network of Master Trainers blankets the globe from Russia to Rio.

Like the age-old battle between good and evil, sales and marketing coexist, yet can't live without the other. And to use baseball as an analogy, marketing would be the starting pitcher, while sales would be the closer—the player whose job is to complete the game with a win.

I've used Jay's ideas to land appointments with prospects in wildly imaginative ways. I once mailed a coconut to an elusive CFO from a major hospital. Written on it in black marker: "You're a tough nut to crack." Got the meeting. I've given a cactus to a rude, dragonlike government employee and told her that it reminded me of her personality. Risky move? She laughed hysterically and gave me documents on the spot that normally took two weeks to receive. Just as good salespeople need guts to go on, good marketers need guts to boldly bring their products and services to the attention of their target market.

So you can join associations and networking groups. You can buy memorable products and advertising specialties to gain attention. You can form strategic alliances and create unique offerings. These strategies will all get you discovered by the media, and uncovered by prospects.

But if You Can't Close Them, All Your Marketing Efforts Are Worthless

That is the 800-pound lie of Guerrilla Marketing—you do what we teach you, and success comes knocking on your bank account. It's just not true. You need to pair up your marketing strategies with selling skills.

Again, you can get all the leads you can handle, but if you can't convert them from prospects to customers, your lead-generation efforts are worthless.

As proof, read Kathy's story. By believing everyone is a prospect, this guerrilla marketer confuses activity with productivity.

A Sales Moment Frozen in Time

In Kathy's early days selling financial services for a large national bank, any prospect was fresh meat, whether she met them at an association event or pulled them from the bank database or was referred to them by existing customers. If she could find an inexpensive way to promote herself, that defined her preferred marketing activity.

So she was aggressively working the local chamber of commerce for leads when Kathy first contacted this business owner. The experience, for her, is frozen in time.

Have you ever been to a meatpacking business?

Maybe you'd call it a slaughterhouse.

Either way, you don't really want to wear an expensive linen suit into this environment. But you do want to tour a prospect's business.

It was disgusting: 15-foot-long cow intestines hanging on walls. Other parts that she didn't want to know about hung or were stacked in coolers. And slippery floors everywhere. But at least the owner tried to keep her off those surfaces.

And the smell? Okay, revolting. Kathy could have skipped that memory.

And then she was asked, "Do you want to see the meat lockers?" What to do? The answer is always yes. So in she went—high heels and all.

Everything was frozen, including her.

Stars! She's looking at the ceiling and there are stars everywhere. This is kind of cool. Then she realizes that she's lying on her back and the stars are moving around because her head has just hit the floor, quite hard.

After that, all Kathy remembers is that the owner didn't want to move his money to the bank and to bring flat shoes to wear around hazardous prospects. And she remembered the lump was on her skull for about three weeks before it disappeared.

Postmortem: Aside from our theme of combat wounds (which you'll notice more of throughout the book), Kathy realized that marketing efforts can be expensive, time-consuming, even painful when they don't result in a sale. Should you choose to create unique marketing plays (and you should because they are, perhaps, the most fun, most creative part of business-building practices), make sure that you are playing with and to your exact target market. Remember that prequalifying, disqualifying, and qualifying should be part of your lead-generation design process. This is exactly where too many Guerrilla Marketing efforts go bad. Your big effort, your advertising or telemarketing splash, dumps too many prospects into the sales funnel, thus leaving you to wade through many, many bad ones to find a few good ones. And with those good ones, your sales stories don't even get interesting unless you have the persuasion skills to advance prospects beyond qualifying. You'll only get the fairy-tale ending when you can actually close someone. The key truth here is that

your selling skills make marketing efforts worthwhile. And you will continue to gain sales strategy
and technique ideas throughout the rest of this book.

● ● ●

Two lessons we gather from the 800-pound lie of
Guerrilla Marketing:

1. Market to the perfect prospect.

2. Bring to the party the ability to close them.

Both these factors come from work you do prior to
your arrival. Marketing smart is related to the design of
your programs. Closing is related to (gulp) training. If
you can't close before you generate leads, you won't suddenly find the skills when you arrive at the slaughterhouse. Develop your sales talent today. If you need to, go
get training. This can keep you, like Kathy, from being
frozen out of a new customer's life.

Dairy Queen • Wrap-Up

Your ability to disqualify quickly will eliminate the
#1 problem salespeople face. It's all about good decision
making. List five things that you absolutely require in
order to begin the selling process with your prospects.
Write them out in the form of questions you would use

during the call. Do you need to find out about money? Who are the decision makers? Is there an urgent need? How many follow-up phone calls will you tolerate before walking away? Make money faster and easier when you sell by deciding today how to quickly Dairy Queen prospects.

    1.

    2.

    3.

    4.

    5.

CHAPTER THREE

Good Versus Evil

Old School Is Closed

Playing for Prospects

How's this selling stunt for a memorable moment? Your author and collector of blunders pulled this off when he was a sales newbie. The lesson, though, is useful for any salesperson.

It was our industry's biggest trade show, and I was a rookie working the booth for my company. NACE, the National Association of Colleges and Employers, serves almost 4,000 organizations—schools and the companies that recruit at them.

I wanted to make a good first impression and had had a great show, even recommending a unique strategy to bring traffic to the booth, making me a temporary hero.

At the event's big dinner, 3,000 people filled the ballroom of the Hyatt Crown Center in Kansas City. A jazz band was playing, and two incredible buffet tables ran wall to wall on either side of the room. Food covered the white tablecloths, and decorations included festive streamers, candles, and brightly polished musical instruments.

As a trumpet player who had to choose between basketball and band in college, I had long ago set aside my horn. But I was feeling on top of the world, and the temptation was too great. There were two temptations, actually. One was the trumpet, and the other was a table of good-looking women I'd met during the conference. I grabbed a shiny instrument off the buffet, knelt down next to the table of women, and started to play. Fifty feet away, the band's drummer saw me and started to call me up on the stage. That was a bit more attention than I wanted, so I grinned, shook my head no, and turned back to return the horn.

As I replaced the trumpet in the display, it dragged streamers across some of the candles. The spectacular centerpiece of brass instruments on the buffet table was now in flames. In the darkened room, the fire was actually quite beautiful. I began beating on it with the tablecloths. Waiters rushed over with water pitchers, dumping water on the fire and finally extinguishing the inferno.

And the band played on.

The evening continued without interruption. Waiters began cleaning up my mess, and people along the buffet table began laughing. I was relieved that the ceilings were so high that no alarms had sounded and (this would have been fun) sprinklers had not drenched 3,000 of my new friends. Thankfully, nothing really bad happened—that is, until my VP of sales heard about my performance.

_____ **Postmortem**: Looking back on that experience made me wonder, What is a salesperson? Someone crying for attention? *Look at me, listen to me, love me. Buy from me!* Sometimes we just need to sell and shut up. We did gain clients, prospects, and great exposure from that show. I didn't need to go beyond the call of duty and try to be the shining star (by the way, my VP was furious, but I bailed myself out with plenty of business from the event).

Here's the real trouble revealed by my magnificent mistake:

Old school is closed!

Traditional feature-and-benefit selling doesn't work as well as it used to. What we grew up with and how we learned to "pitch prospects" is rarely useful anymore. Let's first have a one-sentence definition of that classic feature/benefit sales approach so we're all on the same page. *Feature/benefit selling is where we offer a laundry list of all the good things prospects will experience when they buy from us.*

One of the problems with this approach is that it gives us the tendency to talk too much. We play the numbers game, spitting out benefits, hoping one will strike a chord and cause the buyer to buy.

As we look at the sales blunders in this chapter, think about whether you are using old, even ancient, selling techniques to move prospects to buy. One of the great reasons to sell beyond features and benefits is that you distinguish yourself from all the old sales dogs hounding buyers all day long.

Funny thing, too, about this sales approach we grew up with is that it makes us work harder than we should. Shouldn't the buyer be doing most of the talking?

How well do you use silence to sell? Do you work hard to say nothing, at the proper times, during your presentation? Ask great questions. State your case. Get out of the way, and you'll help your buyer buy better than before.

● ● ●

One of my favorite tales comes from a woman rep using an ancient strategy that backfires badly. Her approach was first recommended in a book written in 1935 . . .

The Ghost of Dale Carnegie

It started out so smoothly. Carol had generated a good lead and called on the company to discuss handling its insurance needs. The office manager really had her act together, giving her all the information she needed to submit to insurance carriers and get the quotes. Carol drafted the proposal and went to meet the female business owner to offer her choices.

Everything continued well. The numbers were good, and the prospect was giving her good buying signals. Carol was aware of the woman executive's unusual last name and decided to try her Dale Carnegie *How to Win Friends and Influence People* strategy. You might be familiar with the fact that Carnegie wrote that people's names are the most precious thing in the world to them. Questions about people's names can be quite flattering. There is often a fascinating story behind there. Maybe the family came to America from a foreign country. Perhaps an ancestor was someone famous.

"I have a friend, Donna—my absolute best friend in the world—with the same unique last name as yours. Could you two be related?" Carol asked. Her big smile invited the prospect to share some personal information.

The woman glared at her, and her words went cold. "That is my husband's ex-wife."

In Carol's mind alarm bells rang, lights flashed.

Across the desk a voice said, "We'll get back to you." And of course she never did.

Postmortem: Poor Carol, she basically said, "Hey, my best friend used to sleep with your husband. Wanna do business with me?" Reality here is this—old school is closed.

And there she was, in first place, goal line in sight, and she stumbles over an old technique. Perhaps the DNA of all salespeople is embedded (infected?) with these old techniques, this dinosaur disease. Here's what to do until you discover a cure (you could find yours in several places inside these pages). Find ways to distinguish yourself from others who compete with you. Be determined to be unique, and prospects will remember you in a crowd. They might even look forward to your visit.

I was speaking at a Sales & Marketing Executives International event and a guy who'd been in sales for 50 years yelled out during my presentation, "You're right! The stuff I used to do doesn't work anymore!" The audience and I then began to collect the names of "old-world" closes. You remember the alternate choice, reduce to the ridiculous, impending event. How about the "porcupine close?" This is where you stick the buyer on his or her "closing question":

"Do you have it in red?"
"If I can get it in red, right now, will you buy it?"

Trouble is buyers have experienced these closes for decades.

These old techniques are no longer techniques but tricks. And nobody likes to be tricked.

Your ability to let the prospect do the work on a sales call will help you better listen and observe. Ask intelligent, nonmanipulative questions and this can help you attain sales nirvana.

● ● ●

Here is another old-fashioned mistake of my own, committed so early in the sales process I didn't even get to try any closes . . .

Enough to Make a Grown Man Cry

"I lost my rep on the South Side of Chicago," the medical products sales manager told me on the phone. He asked me to meet him at a trade show to discuss using my search skills to fill the position. My search fee would be about $12,000. I was really glad to meet at a trade show, since I could walk around and try to get more business from other companies exhibiting there.

The manager wasn't at the booth, but three of his reps were—two middle-aged women, and a guy about 24 years old. "I'm here to meet John," I told them. They asked what I did, and I made one of the dumbest mistakes of my career. "Oh, I'm a medical sales recruiter, and John wants me to help find a rep for your open territory—on the South Side of Chicago." Dead silence, shocked looks, and suddenly one of the reps bursts into tears, runs about 20 feet away, and starts sobbing uncontrollably. It was the guy.

"Way to go, you jerk," one of the women said. "That's his territory. He had no idea he was being fired, until now."

I felt my heart plunge to the bottom of my belly. The manager had said the territory was open and the rep was gone. I walked over and tried to apologize to the guy, explaining my lack of information about him. He was cool, but he left the show, and wasn't at the booth a few minutes later when his boss arrived.

The manager was furious! Of course it was all my fault. He demanded that I find the replacement—for free. I left there completely disgusted with myself and without a signed contract. Then I had to explain the whole story to my boss. Nothing as fun as reliving your costly mistakes to the guy who manages you, coaches you, and can ultimately fire you.

Postmortem: What a horrible experience for me. I learned that all those sales books and tapes that tell you to promote yourself at every possible opportunity are sometimes wrong. I suggest you keep your mouth shut until you're in front of the decision maker. If you want to make small talk, fine. But why try to resell yourself to everyone you meet? Your appointment with the decision maker is already secured. If others ask who you are, simply say that you're an industry service provider who's been asked to sit down with your boss. Then get on another topic.

● ● ●

In this next story, Megan learns the most expensive lesson I've ever come across in 600+ selling mistakes . . .

Sales Pitcher Strikes Out on Megadeal

Megan decided to sit in on a nationally known sales trainer's program—just in case she could acquire some ideas on how to significantly increase her effectiveness in selling.

During a conversation with the expert, she claimed to understand the concept of "unpaid consulting." This is the process of dumping extremely valuable insights, even complex solutions, in front of a potential client before a relationship has been established. Megan agreed that unpaid consulting happens at times, but also believed her sales education was correct in that both showing off and being thorough were a big part of designing proposals.

Also, Megan was involved in a big deal, and she just knew this guy was wrong about how to prepare and present proposals. She went ahead and made a very detailed proposal on a $64 million project. Her personal commission on the deal was $3.5 million!

They loved her proposal. In fact they accepted it.

But they bought the stuff from someone else. She later discovered that the company took apart her proposal and used it to craft their ideal solution. They then began contacting companies in a lower price range than hers and farming out the pieces of her artistically crafted ideas.

Megan will always wonder who got her multimillion-dollar commission check.

Postmortem: When you have a great month, you might reward yourself with a gift or some extra personal time—a vacation trip to an island perhaps. How would you treat yourself after a $3.5 million bonus check? Megan never got to find out. She got suckered by a prospect who wanted to siphon her knowledge and shop her solution to someone cheaper. Be very careful before creating a "work of art" proposal of high quality and detail. Get very comfortable with your potential client before investing all that time and ink. You might just find yourself writing fewer proposals—and spending more pure selling time on higher-probability prospects.

If the nature of your business is to draft documents to present to buyers, you want to think long and hard on this question: *Do your proposals allow prospects to steal your brainpower?*

Buyers have learned long ago that salespeople are suckers for individuals who are interested in getting written quotes for business. These buyers know, as do many sales managers, that too often reps are dreamers and will play the numbers game. This means salespeople will offer complex solutions in the hope that prospects might buy.

Reality reveals that this old approach of drafting documents for everyone who nods his or her head or grunts into a telephone is foolish and expensive. Many of these buyers want a peek at your data to solve problems themselves or to check prices or even to keep current vendors in line by threatening to change suppliers. This is deception, pure and simple. And as the late, great sales guru David Sandler once noted, "You can lie to a salesperson and still get into heaven."

The lesson here is that preparing proposals can waste lots of time showboating in print for prospects who have no intention of doing business with you.

● ● ●

The trouble is we were taught to believe that selling was about benefits when, today, *selling is about change*. We need to *unlearn* benefits as our sole strategy and realize that our job is really to create change or help motivate our prospects to change.

So how do we get them to change vendors, change their financial strategies, change their minds?

Psychologists and business experts know that a specific method is used to create change in an individual or an organization. This method is known as the change formula.

The following formula was made famous by Massachusetts Institute of Technology Sloan School of Management professor Edgar Schein. He was given the prestigious American Society of Training and Development (ASTD) Lifetime Achievement Award in May 2000. This means your sales training peers recognize the value of the magic of this idea.

The Change Formula

$$C = D \times V \times F > S$$

In other words, people will **Change (C)** once they

1. are aware of their **Dissatisfaction (D)** or frustration with their current situation;

2. are given a **Vision (V)** for what the future could look and feel like;

3. are offered the First Steps **(F)** to transition to that vision; and

4. realize that the Dissatisfaction, Vision, and First Steps are greater motivators than their Status Quo **(S)**, or their current situation.

Notice that a key factor in helping change occur is not benefits, but frustration or dissatisfaction. This huge hint says that people are motivated, not by the good things, but by the bad things that could affect their business or personal lives.

Let's be clear on our definition of feature/benefit selling. This is where we basically offer a laundry list of all the good things that will happen when a prospect buys from us. We trust that something on that list will trigger a buying response and we'll end up with a new client. Problem is, it makes us talk too much—like the mechanic who says, "I couldn't fix your brakes, so I made your horn a little louder."

Keep the change formula in mind when you sell. It should remind you that the purpose of your call is to focus conversations on each piece of this change puzzle—whether the prospect is standing still financially, moving backward, or making progress.

In the wrap-up of this chapter, you'll learn a method that honors the tradition of feature/benefit selling while offering an alternative approach that works—to motivate prospects to change.

● ● ●

But first, in this final tale, an incredibly dense, old-school sales guy pitches until his prospect is physically debilitated. And after this bizarre blunder, you'll be led into a smart strategy that you can use now to sell more . . .

Prospect Fades to Black as Sales Rep Rambles

JP's father was the only real estate agent in a small town in Canada. After school, the young man went to work with him for a few years. Those years were enough to teach JP that selling was not meant for him.

His father had a client who would buy run-down houses, renovate them a little, and rent them for a small profit. This client came in one day to talk to the father, who quickly ushered him into the closing room. As was his habit, Dad left the door open so that the rest of the agents could see and hear what a real closer was like.

Now, JP's father had a habit of rambling on and on and on. This day was no different, and, as the afternoon wore on, it appeared that Dad was trying to set the world rambling record. After two hours of glancing into the room and listening, JP realized that he had not heard the client speak at all. The gentleman simply gazed out the window, nodding occasionally. The Realtor's son stepped into the office, hoping to save this unfortunate soul from any more of his father's prattling, when he noticed that the client was slumped in the chair. His color was ashen.

Unknown to anyone in the office, Dad's client was diabetic and had lapsed into a semiconscious state. Emergency care was immediately summoned, and the client ended up being released from the hospital after a few days.

The old Realtor later admitted that he'd realized the client had become unresponsive. However (and this is the scary part), he chalked it up to the need to do more "selling."

Postmortem: Think of that poor prospect's last image as his world faded to black—a salesman's mouth motoring along. God save us from long-winded salespeople!

●   ●   ●

What if we had an alternative to benefit-based selling? Another option to the idea that the more information you toss out there, the more likely some points will make an impression and cause the sale to close. I don't call that selling, I call it *hoping.*

I confess that I have contributed to this problem by helping fill up the world with schizophrenic sales reps.

In 1988 I had 15 sales reps working for me: men, women; big, small; funny, serious; married, single, divorced; lousy dressers, clotheshorses; coffee, water, and cola drinkers.

Each one was required to come to work, hit their ON button, then parrot my sales script to hundreds of people every day. Regardless of who they were, they became MINE when they sold. Their style was a reflection of my beliefs, standards, and desires about pitching and responding to objections. I had effectively manufactured sales reps with multiple personalities by requiring that they leave themselves outside the door and adopt another persona (designed and dictated by me) to sell. They came, every day, to my Island of Dr. Moreau in Glenview, Illinois, and turned into sales monsters.

This was bad decision making at its finest.

One day I stood, watched, and listened to the chorus of sales songs being sung across our phone lines. My creations were acting just as I'd taught them to. But I no longer felt the happy papa, the proud professor. I caught my general manager's eye, and she followed me into my office.

"All of them pitch prospects the same," I said. "Do you think it's annoying to our market audience that we and hundreds of competitors in Chicago say the exact thing on every call?"

Our team made about 1,000 phone calls a day. So was our base of prospects hearing tens of thousands of identical pitches all day? How can buyers decide which firm to use? How do we distinguish ourselves that way? Hope we get lucky and catch someone in their moment of dire need? Gamble that the sheer numbers will generate a return on effort?

She shrugged and nodded, her reply echoing my fears.

I went home that evening, determined to heal my team of the disease of my poor decision making.

I radically changed our phone script.

For one week I made phone calls myself, trying out some new language. Every one of us had been raised on traditional feature/benefit selling. In fact, our corporate office had trained more than 500 locations to use traditional sales thinking, because there wasn't another option. I was determined to abandon it, simply because everyone else was using it.

During that week I had deeper prospecting conversations than I'd ever had. I landed a very satisfying, highly profitable sale and called a company meeting for the following Monday.

Nobody worked that morning. I ran the new scripts by the team and explained the concepts behind using them. We did an exercise I designed to teach these concepts and anchor the new learning. Everyone was happy, perhaps even relieved, to try something new.

We doubled our sales in a month.

An amazing transformation shaped our team!

Instead of talking heads repeating our benefits for anyone we could land on the phone, we had *customized conversations* with each decision maker.

Our salespeople weren't exhausted from playacting every day. In fact, they were energized by these dialogues.

Everyone found it was suddenly fun to sell.

Here's the secret to the new approach.

It's based on the age-old battle between good and evil.

We grew up with what is now considered an "old-school" approach to selling. We used to use good things to attract buyers. However, the change formula tells us that frustration or bad things that happen (or are about to happen) are more effective motivators than good. So instead of talking to prospects about benefits, we'll talk about problems or the consequences or the current path they're traveling on.

This is so easy to do that you'll wonder why you didn't think of this many years and many more lost prospects ago. There are three steps to this. An example follows.

1. *Take a sheet of paper. Draw a line down the middle. Write "Benefits" over the left side and "Problems" over the right.* On the left side, list all the good things that customers gain from your product or service. On the right side, list all the trouble that customers deal with—until your product or service fixes them. These are the problems you solve.

So, "Benefits" is all about the wonderful things that make businesses successful and enjoyable. This turns happy prospects into delighted clients. "Problems" is about the vile, unpleasant, nasty parts of doing business. These are the surprises that ambush our prospects and take them offtrack.

A simple way to compile this (as if it could be simpler) is to use your company brochures. Look at all your benefits shown, then write down the opposite of each (problems) on your page. You'll find that some of the benefits have many opposites.

Here's an example from the automotive industry for selling a new car:

GOOD STUFF

(Sales Pitch—benefits to offer)
- You'll love the prestige of owning a new car.
- This baby rides and handles like a dream.
- The six-speaker sound system is fantastic!
- This has air bags everywhere, all the latest safety features.
- We offer a 100-year warranty.

PROBLEMS

(Prospect's Thinking—troubles to solve)
- Embarrassed to drive older model in front of my company, clients, and prospects
- My current car is not fun to drive—it runs and sounds like it's old.
- I'd like to use CDs in my car, rather than a bunch of old cassettes.
- I'm nervous putting my small kids into this older car.
- I'm surprised and frustrated when problems pop up with this vehicle.

2. *On another page, craft a list of questions that point prospects to the problem-solving capabilities of your products and services.* You will want to ask a couple of these questions early in the conversation. The variety in your list is important because different salespeople, with different personalities, will choose a question they are most comfortable asking, perhaps based on their knowledge or expertise or experience in solving that problem. This is where selling becomes fun. This is where you begin to generate those customized conversations.

3. *Put it into play.* Ask one of these questions of a prospect and see where the conversation takes the two of you. The deeper you dig, the better you help that person see the danger of trouble breaking down his or her plans and dreams for success.

I encourage you to do this exercise with a team of reps in your office. If you're an entrepreneur, get together with your networking group or other business professionals and work through this concept on each of their businesses as well as yours. When I first used this exact exercise at a car dealership, I returned a week later to some great stories of reps who were not only having better dialogues with prospects, but were earning quicker closes as well. One salesman asked a man who wandered into the store during the day if he sold for a living.

On getting a yes, the rep said, "Can I ask you a question? Are you ever embarrassed to have prospects see your car?"

The buyer launched into a story about his strategy for parking his old beater vehicle far from the front of a business he was calling on. He didn't want his prospects to see his car, or worse, to expect the prospect to ride with him, should they go to lunch.

This man who wandered into a car dealership was suffering from the evil impact of his old, beat-up automobile. The rep I had trained focused in on the bad, rather than the benefits. And in his words, "I closed that guy faster than anyone I'd ever dealt with."

This approach works—and I want to leave you with an old joke that reinforces the ideas you've learned here.

Lieutenant Miller was assigned to the Army enlistment center, where he advised new recruits about their government benefits, especially their insurance.

Before long, Captain Smith noticed that Lieutenant Miller had a near-100-percent record for insurance sales. Everyone Miller spoke to bought additional coverage. This had never happened before. Rather than ask about it, the captain stood in the back of the room and listened to Miller's sales pitch.

Miller explained the basics of the insurance to the new recruits, and then said, "If you have U.S. armed services insurance and go into battle and are killed, the government has to pay a quarter-million dollars to your beneficiaries. If you don't have this additional insurance, and you go into battle and get killed, the government only has to pay a maximum of six thousand."

"Now," he concluded, "which bunch do you think they're going to send into battle first?"

See how the salesman points to problems on the horizon for his prospects? His key question is a powerful motivation tool.

Enforce a ban on schizophrenic salespeople. You don't have to adopt a new personality to sell. Take the time to craft your perfect pitch. It's like giving yourself a healthy raise.

Good Versus Evil • Wrap-Up

Your ability to be flexible when you sell is critical to closing a higher percentage of prospects. The Benefits vs. Problems exercise is best done with your salesforce, perhaps at a weekly staff meeting. For entrepreneurs and independent reps, get with your networking or some accountability group and design five bullet points that present your benefits and five that present the problems you solve. Use this to increase your ability to have high-impact conversations with potential clients.

Good Stuff

(Benefits to offer)

1.

2.

3.

4.

5.

Problems

(Troubles to solve)

1.

2.

3.

4.

5.

CHAPTER FOUR

Respect and Revenge

Calculating Clients and Conniving Reps

Perfect Pitch

Jill's presentation is music, except to her prospect's ears. She was excited to start her sales career at a big copier company—one that had the best sales training in the industry and was known as an organization that gave great support to its reps.

Jill's sales manager enforced one particular rule: Reps do not go on sales calls alone until they have *memorized* their presentation, word for word. She stayed up late at night and read the script over and over and over. During the day, she would ride with experienced reps or her manager to learn selling skills from the pros in action.

Repeatedly, Jill stood before her sales manager and practiced her pitch. Inevitably, she'd blow some part of it and be told, "Keep working on it. See you later." One day Jill finally nailed it. Her manager smiled and said, "Looks like you're ready to solo!"

That day she was as nervous as if on a blind date (a perfect description of most first sales calls). Standing before a businessman, Jill began to speak. The memorized script was perfectly burned into her brain.

But something was wrong, and she couldn't quite figure it out. Then it hit her. She felt both humiliated and stupid when she realized what she'd done. Throughout the presentation she had been calling the businessman— just as the script read—"Mr. Prospect."

Postmortem: Jill's blunder should help you think about how you look at, and treat, your prospects. Do you respect them as individuals? You show respect by working to discover their exact needs and then to address those needs before switching on your autopilot. By contrast, do prospects view you as an individual? How do you strive to be memorable, standing out from thousands of sales animals badgering buyers each day?

If you think enough about this, you'll realize the word *respect* embodies everything that is wrong and right about the world of selling.

● ● ●

Do you see each of your prospects differently? Enjoy the imagery from the next story (and don't let your kids read this one over your shoulder) . . .

Eye on Sales

Lousy prospects! Tom was headed to the Midwest on a ride with his Indiana/Michigan rep for some sales coaching during calls. His biggest prospect was a large hospital, but the buyer had the secretary say he was not available when they arrived. The gutless buyer actually hid in his office, his presence betrayed by his coughing fit, heard clearly from his supposedly empty office.

"Okay, man. What's next?" Tom said, "Let's cold-call somebody."

The rep suddenly lit up. "There is a place near here we can visit."

And this is how Tom discovered Naked City.

This nudist colony was more of a club than a camp. The owner was extremely wealthy. They walked up a long, beautifully landscaped path toward a geodesic dome. The building was one-way glass, dark from the outside. Inside, a car that had belonged to Elvis sat in the lobby.

"Tom," the rep said. "Don't look at me. If you look at me, I'll start laughing."

The sales manager had no idea what his rep was talking about until the receptionist stood up to greet them—completely nude.

The inside of the building was glass in every direction. The two men could see "uniformed" office workers everywhere—if skin could be considered an outfit. The most clothing they saw was a pair of shoes on a man's feet.

The owner's elderly mother (horrors!) invited the salesmen to sit down in the boardroom. The large table was clear glass, so, again, you could see everything about the other person, except whether they wanted to buy or not.

Then, as if this whole scene wasn't memorable enough, two women and a man walked into a room behind the prospect and climbed on a large trampoline. Evidently they exercised before lunch and the visitors got to, or had to, watch while they were pitching their food-service equipment products.

The mother and her kitchen manager placed a small order—hardly worth the gas and time spent for a national sales manager and his regional rep.

But you can be sure that memory is burned into Tom's brain for eternity. And the story made the rounds twice at the company, circling a second time after the delivery driver made his visit.

Postmortem: Tom sees prospects as never before! Interesting sales scenario. Unique; in fact, I get so many "thank God that didn't happen to me" stories that this might be just the opposite; "Gee, I wish I were there." Here's a related thought to the tale: Can you look inside someone without seeing the outside? One of your greatest skills as a sales pro is the ability to dig inside the mind of a prospect without being distracted by outward appearances. Keep your focus and zero in with good questions, and you could sell anybody the shirt off their back (well almost anybody).

● ● ●

In this story an entrepreneur's words speak louder than he planned. And his lack of appreciation for a customer converts her to an ex-customer . . .

Auto Shop Drives Away Customer

The woman arrived at the shop for some minor car work, and a mechanic discovered that she needed more serious repairs.

The car was up on the rack, but she insisted on calling her husband before she incurred more charges. Mike, the store manager, called the man, who immediately flew into a rage. "You auto shop guys are a bunch of thieves. Just because a woman comes in, you try to rip her off. There better really be something wrong with our car."

The office was separated from the customer waiting area by a soundproof glass door. Mike turned to the shop's owner and began telling him what a jerk this guy was. He had ranted about the husband for a couple of minutes when a knock on the door interrupted. It was the wife.

She stared at the owner and manager for a brief moment and said, "I can read lips. Take my car off your rack. I'm leaving." She drove away while the two men were still in shock. She had "heard" every insulting comment Mike had made.

Postmortem: Mike and his boss learned a lesson about respect. If you always treat prospects and customers (and friends!) with respect, you'll develop a reputation as a courteous professional service provider. It doesn't matter if that frustrating person is present or not, a good attitude toward them will keep your heart and mind and business healthier. Show respect before and behind everyone you work with.

● ● ●

Showing disrespect isn't always verbal, either. In this story, a company's beautifully designed newsletter slanders people from a certain city—and proves that the printed word can be both expensive and costly.

New Yorkers Need Not Send Money

Lisa had taken a new job working for a very high-end marketing design literature firm. "Communication arts" some call it. During the first few months, her boss worked on Lisa to enter her contact list into the company e-mail database so he could send these new contacts his weekly newsletter. She was understandably resistant. Lisa had spent years developing these relationships. She was hesitant to give away all her contacts. And she wasn't certain that the weekly corporate e-mail would help her sell. Eventually the owner wore her down, and Lisa's hard-earned names were dumped into the company database.

The following week the newsletter opened with *"I hate New York: Everyone I have ever met from New York has been rude and obnoxious."* Her (rude and obnoxious) boss also pointed out that he had never been to New York, his opinion was based on his own personal experiences with New Yorkers, and he stated that he didn't want any angry calls or e-mails sent to him as a result of this article.

The first phone call Lisa received was from the CEO of a company who had her $100,000 proposal sitting on her desk. In her Brooklyn accent, she informed Lisa that she would be taking her business elsewhere. A close friend and former employer called next and asked, again in her New York accent, that she be reimbursed for the free displays she'd given Lisa's company—to furnish trade show booths. It continued in that same vein for the rest of the morning. Had it never occurred to the owner that people from New York had feelings?!

And this wasn't his first insensitive correspondence. He'd previously quoted Hitler in a newsletter! Now his ignorance of the basic fundamentals of corporate communication had ruined relationships again.

Lisa's boss had managed to wreck the heart of her contact base, destroying serious sales opportunities. She immediately began her hunt for a new job.

Postmortem: Egos are like big termites that eat away at the structure of a business relationship. They might be the #1 factor in the collapse of business deals. Most ego trouble comes from an individual who has little respect for people he works with and prospects he talks with all day long. Someone who thinks they can get away with attitudes and actions like this is usually unaware of the scope of the real damage. Lisa heard from a small portion of those insulted. As you can imagine, many, many more were probably irritated by this and said nothing— they just quietly went away. Keep your ego in check and show respect to everyone, even if you think you have something cute or witty to say.

● ● ●

Another form of respect involves withholding the truth from people. Neal learns that lying to prospects can have a sobering effect on potential customers and a spirit-wrenching impact on himself . . .

Hotel Surprise Guest

Neal was the sales manager for a boutique hotel with a lot of charm located in the heart of the city's entertainment district.

He was new to selling in the hospitality industry, so Neal was eager to bring in business. But a few months of frustration were costing the man money. The biggest problem was losing accounts due to the fact that the immediate area was known for crime.

Neal decided to ask for some direction from his general manager on how exactly to handle this topic when potential clients brought it up. The GM advised, "Look them straight in the face and tell them 'I'm not aware of a problem in this area. That's news to me.'"

Okay, interesting way to handle trouble. But the young sales manager thanked him and thought about how he would use that line on his next prospect.

Two weeks later (and wiser), Neal was introduced to a couple who wanted to book their daughter's wedding party at the property. This was midmorning, so Neal suggested talking to them in the hotel bar that looked out

on the street. After about 30 minutes, the father of the
bride asked the question that Neal had been waiting for:
"Everything seems to be perfect; however, my only concern is the crime in this area, and we want our daughter's
wedding party to be safe."

Neal looked him straight in the eye and said, "I'm
not aware of a problem in this area, what exactly are you
referring to?"

Before he could speak, a homeless person who was
sitting, unseen, below the window stood up and, while
singing heartily, attempted to relieve himself on the
glass. Stunned, both the parents and Neal sat in silence.
The hotel bellman rushed over to attempt to remove the
man from the hotel property, but only succeeded in starting a yelling match.

"THAT is what I'm referring to!" shouted the father
of the bride. The young sales manager was flustered. He
really did not know what to do and was embarrassed
that he had lied and tried to deceive the man. Out of his
dry mouth trickled some mumblings and apologies. The
parents finally did have the wedding party at the hotel,
but the shame that arose from that experience changed
both Neal's sales strategy and his conscience.

Postmortem: Neal's pitch suffered the wedding
bell blues. Although he did analyze his mistake quite
well: "Looking back, it was perfectly obvious what I

should have done. When confronted with the question, I should have been perfectly honest. I should have told him, 'Yes, there have been incidents in this area. Let me tell you what the hotel can do to make you and your party more at ease. First, we can add hotel security for the weekend of the wedding. Second, we can reserve our hotel shuttle to transport them anywhere within a 15-mile radius.' Even being honest would not have prevented the homeless person from disrupting my meeting; however, I'm sure I would have felt better about myself after the fact." The lesson here is to be honest with prospects. They want to feel that the choice they are making is the safest bet they can place. Your job is to make them know that you can solve any problems that arise. You are that safest bet— for their money, their reputation, and even their physical well-being. Be honest. Every honest salesperson helps heal that notion that many sales reps are snakes.

● ● ●

If you think enough about this, you'll realize the word *respect* embodies everything that is wrong and right about the world of selling.

I have a friend, Scott, who sold cars when his family owned a Mazda/VW dealership. As soon as the buyer signed for the vehicle, Scott would dramatically hold a finger in the air, smile, and say, "I have something special for you." He'd open his desk drawer, dig out the buyer's gift, and, thanking them for their good decision, hand over a pair of white athletic socks.

Scott told me that he did this for two reasons. First, it made the sale memorable: It was weird enough that buyers would say to friends, "Yeah, I bought a $26,000 car and got a free pair of socks." Second, it was his way of saying that he hated how buyers worked him so hard on price. The $2 pair of socks was his way of saying thanks for the trouble; this is about what you're worth to me.

DANGER: Please do not be tempted to belittle the people that put bread on your table.

On one level I understand how Scott feels. On a higher level, the problem with reps being disrespectful to prospects is compounded by prospects showing massive disrespect for salespeople. They think we're snakes and liars who would never tell our closest friends what we do for a living.

Where does the fault lie in all of this frustration between them and us?

We need to accept responsibility for fixing ourselves first.

Here's something I challenge all reps to dwell on. Prospects often find us difficult to deal with because we think that the signature on our paycheck is the person paying them their money. It isn't. The real signature belongs to that person behind the counter or desk or on the other end of the phone.

If we keep the perspective that prospects or future clients and current customers are signing our checks, we will show respect to all of them. Because we never know in the early stages of our selling relationship which one will actually be paying us, do we? So treat every one as if they were slapping their signature on your paycheck.

● ● ●

However, what about when we've been treated too poorly, too often? That's why it's both fun and necessary to draw attention to the other side of the respect coin. That is our need for . . .

Revenge

Revenge resides on the opposite end of our selling spectrum from respect.

While you should show appreciation for the potential of anyone you call on, there are just some times when you hit your limit. There are customers and prospects who don't treat you respectfully. And they do this over and over. In these situations, sometimes you just can't handle it anymore. You just can't take these evil buyers and pathetic prospects who make your misery their mission.

I applaud when you find ways to creatively blow off steam and at least mentally get even with people. Some fiendish prospects out there work you so hard at selling for a living that a chain gang could seem like a promotion. And let me make it clear that I'm not endorsing retaliation as a strategy. Please don't exact revenge and then use your one phone call from jail to ask me for bond money.

The sales life is tough. It's rough on relationships in particular. Each of us loves to be liked by others, but we can't sell to everyone. Unfortunately, too many of us take this rejection personally. So frustration, disgust, even anger are built into many of our days.

And this is how some of us wander into the arena of revenge. What do we do, right now, with prospects who are running us ragged?

● ● ●

In this next story, Matt has finally reached his limit with a customer . . .

How to Fire a Customer While Taking His Money

Matt's company supplies pizza ingredients to non-franchise pizza stores in the northwestern United States.

The company had a serious problem customer who was only to receive his products after paying the delivery driver in cash. Matt's supply house often had thousands of dollars at risk for busy, privately run restaurants that would string out suppliers for months, before paying or suddenly going out of business. This guy had been sticking it to everyone who supplied him. The word was out not to do business with him.

One of the drivers made the mistake of taking a check from this customer, who was a cash on demand (COD) customer. Of course the check bounced—there were not sufficient funds in the man's bank account.

Revenge came on Labor Day weekend.

In the pizza business, school holidays mean nonstop customers—kids with nothing to do that day. This also means nonstop cash.

Of course, the supply store received that restaurant's big holiday order, and Matt decided to deal with this problem child himself. He put on a uniform and drove the delivery truck to the customer. Walking in with the *previous* receipt, Matt waved it above his head and requested cash before he unloaded the pizza supplies. The owner argued that he paid by check the last time (nice try, buddy), and Matt told him he knew nothing of that and was told only to take cash for today's order. The pizza store owner, who had no clue that the truck driver owned the supply house, grumbled, signed the receipt, and handed over about $1,000 cash, never realizing that he was signing and paying for the *last* order—the one he stiffed Matt on. Matt grinned, thanked him, told him that he'd be right back with his food.

Matt walked out the back door, got in the truck, and drove off.

The customer called a short time later, absolutely furious. He had no time to order food for a three-day weekend and basically could do nothing but serve soda. Other suppliers wouldn't ship to him because of his reputation. The $1,000 Matt had taken prevented the man from even buying supplies at Sam's Club. Matt took the call and said he was surprised one of his drivers would do that and promised to talk to that driver immediately to discover what went wrong. He hung up the phone and told his secretary to just hang up if that restaurant owner ever called back. The customer went out of business shortly afterward.

Postmortem: Matt, I'm standing up applauding you right now. This is a great, gutsy lesson. How many of you sales pros reading this right now have the nerve to fire your worst customers today? It's time to take back your dignity. Get revenge by getting rid of people who are giving you aggravation, stringing out the payment of money due you, even giving you ulcers. The time and attention you free up will be useful in acquiring new customers who appreciate what you offer and pay happily and on time.

● ● ●

Start your new year right now, regardless of today's date. Make a resolution that you will do business only with people who respect you and treat you like a partner.

Do you know the real value of increasing the respect you feel for yourself? Do the right thing. It's time for a change. Don't mess any longer with clients who mess with your head. Give them up; let them give ulcers to the competition.

If you, the reader, are rejoicing in revenge and would like some yourself, there are two resources in the Appendix. *Revenge of the Reps,* a free video game, will help you deal with beastly buyers and pathetic prospects and give you great laughs as well. And an exercise for your sales meeting is also included. Check out *Things You'd Love to Say to Evil Prospects.* These should satisfy your thirst for the blood of prospects, for the time being.

● ● ●

Another of our tales in this chapter comes from a rep and his manager who simply hit the wall after too many bad experiences. This is a true horror story, in every sense of the word . . .

Got Any Goodies to Give?

Ray was selling time-share properties, and, while commissions were high, too many people came for presentations simply to sit for 45 minutes, then collect their free gift.

The gifts ranged from weekend stays at resorts to cash to bowling balls and back up in value to a rare automobile giveaway.

The sales reps ranged from those using persuasive skills to old-style types with heavy-handed battering rams for mouths.

It's too early to tell at the beginning of a presentation whether a prospect is just fishing for gifts or is truly interested in an investment in time-sharing.

But this couple tipped their hand as early as one could imagine. The husband filled out their form. Ray sat opposite the couple and began some friendly chitchat.

"So how long have you two been married?"

"Four years" and "Seven years" came simultaneous answers. "Well, we lived together first a few years," clarified the man.

"How many kids?" Ray asked.

"Two" and "Three" spoke husband and wife. Again the words were spoken simultaneously.

Ray glanced at his manager who was sitting nearby. He shook his head in disgust. This was no married couple. The "husband" even wore a wedding ring.

Ray's manager suddenly spun out of his seat and left the room. Ray's conversation went right to business—

locations, the joy of time-share, the lifetime value of an easy, low-cost investment.

Outside the office, the manager glanced at the couple's paperwork and dialed their home number.

The man's wife answered the phone.

"Hello, this is Mr. Roberts at the Vacation Store. Your husband is here talking to us about vacations, and he is eligible to win a brand-new Jeep Cherokee. However, we need his wife to be present for you two to qualify for the car. And you win a weekend trip at a nice hotel for showing up, even if you don't win the car."

"I had no idea. I'll be right there," the real wife replied.

Twenty minutes later she arrived and was led into an office where her husband and his girlfriend were moments away from receiving their free holiday weekend.

As they say in wartime on the battlefield, "All hell broke loose."

Postmortem: Ray and his boss had encountered one too many horrible prospects. They decided they'd had enough and took their own form of revenge. While I can't endorse their behavior, I can't ignore the opportunity to share the story with other reps. After all, aren't many great stories about conflict really tales of revenge? Great movies as well as classical literature (like *The Count of Monte Cristo*, who exacts revenge for 20 years of anguish, loss, and pain) leave us wanting some balance in the universe, some equality between those who take advantage of the downtrodden. In our case, it's the sales rep.

● ● ●

Respect and Revenge · Wrap-Up

How do you mentally create respect for everyone you call on? Here's the strategy. Think on this: You calculate commissions on people long before you're close to closing. Everyone in selling does this. So put it to good use. Set a value on each individual, and respect their potential to pay you. Simple enough? Every suspect, prospect, and client has a dollar value. Consider this hidden value and keep it right in front of you as you sell. Respect will pervade your attitude all day long.

First let me remind you again that the signature on your paycheck is not the person paying you for a living. It's the prospect across the table or down the phone line from you.

I'll give you a trick for valuing everyone you deal with—that is, until you are absolutely sure that you are going to turn your back on them and move on, or until you convert them into customers.

You know how you calculate commissions on people long before you're close to closing? You know what I mean. This person is worth about a sale of X dollars, so my commission would be around Y bucks. You do it; we all do it.

Let's use that to our advantage. Set a value, whatever it is to you, on everyone you meet. Respect their potential to pay you, when you exercise the sales skills to earn their money.

But until you close them, keep in mind how much they are really worth. This will give you the perspective of respect and teach you to treat everyone as someone special, as someone who can feed your family.

CHAPTER FIVE

Crash on Contact

Failed First Impressions

Sales Exhaustion

Joel is a workaholic. Aside from his workplace, he has an office at home in Denver, Colorado. This means Joel is always working, calling East Coast prospects and clients before going to work, and doing paperwork after getting home. He is a hermit, a recluse, and none of his friends have seen him in six months.

One evening Joel received phone calls from everyone he knows. "What is wrong with you, Joel? Have you given up on bars and all the good stuff that comes inside them—music, beer, women?" So with the threat of total abandonment by his buddies, he took a cab to meet them—and made up for six months of alcohol abstinence in one night.

At 3 AM, bleary-eyed and blitzed, Joel staggered into his home. Out of habit, he wandered right into the office. The drunken rep grabbed the phone and called his biggest prospect—a company that spends a quarter of a million dollars on its yearly sales conference. Joel had not yet spoken to the executive but wisely figured that a message from a confident vendor would be a good way to start the man's day and serve as an excellent introduction.

Sputtering and slobbering into the mouthpiece, he pitched, "Oh, please, you've got to buy from me. We're the best. And you're the biggest company I've ever called on. I can do a great job, I swear. Besides, my commission on this project would be beyond belief. Please use me for your event planning. We're the best. You've got to give me a chance." Joel passed out on his desk. The annoying dial tone from the disconnected phone didn't even register on his flatlining brain waves.

There was only one phone call for him the next day, but Joel missed it because he was hung over at home. It was the executive, "Uh, Joel, I believe it was you that called my office at three in the morning. Please don't call me or our company again."

Postmortem: So, this prospect passed out of Joel's life as quickly as Joel passed out on his desk. That prospect probably saved Joel's voice mail and shared it with everyone: "Listen to this sales idiot."

Perhaps it is even floating around the Internet somewhere.

Joel likely didn't share this experience with anyone, until he broke down, sobbing out his story during the "confession session" of one of my speaking programs. Okay, he wasn't sobbing, but he did learn this important lesson—*rest is a weapon*. Robert Ludlum fans will recognize that maxim from his bestselling novels that sprung from *The Bourne Identity*. You get stronger and better at what you do when you regularly back out of your business life to rest and recover. You can attack your market with precision and power only if, and when, you have the energy to do so.

No category of sales horror stories has a total number of tales larger than "first impressions."

The trouble simply centers on this: What do you do when you first walk into a stranger's office? Or connect by phone?

Our great hope at the initial contact with potential customers is that this could be something big— big company, big commission, big boost to our esteem. However, reps can show up tired or unprepared, or sometimes they just get sandbagged by the unexpected.

● ● ●

Selling Mom plus New Baby Equals . . .

Donna's brand-new baby girl had filled her diaper and was screaming hysterically, so she pulled over in the SUV and changed her daughter in the backseat.

A new mom, Donna was exhausted all the time.

As a successful sales pro, she'd given birth to her daughter and was immediately back on the streets meeting clients and prospects.

The rep would wake up early (after waking up throughout the night), feed her precious little one, pack a diaper bag, bundle up the baby, and drop her off at a home-based daycare service.

That kid/dirty diaper/clean diaper juggling act in the car was making Donna late for her first appointment. She raced into the babysitter's house, handed over her daughter and diaper bag, then raced back onto the street to make the meeting.

Can you imagine how sleep deprivation would make anyone prone to mistakes? Donna only made one mistake that morning—she handed the daycare provider her black purse instead of the black diaper bag. A simple mistake, right? Sure, except she didn't realize it until ten minutes into her first appointment, when both Donna and her prospect noticed the smell.

At this point, Donna thought, Is that stupendous stink coming from my bag? What a dummy I am. And what did I feed her last night?

It was awful. The rep could not get in rapport with the prospect—who must have felt assaulted by the smell as well. No sale, of course.

　　__**Postmortem**__: This story reminded me how badly I miss changing diapers, now that my kids are old enough to fall out of trees. Here's a question intended to make you feel guilty: Are you getting enough sleep every night? Your effectiveness during the weekday is closely related to your ability to get your best rest—deep sleep. So turn off the TV, set down the book, leave the bar. Do whatever it takes to put proper sleep back into your schedule and you'll perform better in front of prospects.

● ● ●

Because I speak at so many national sales conferences, I meet reps who are recovering every morning from a late night out. Partying is a big part of these events. However, midweek partying can have a very bad effect on our paycheck . . .

Sunburn Ends Buyer/Seller Relationship

He was an evil buyer. You know the type who tortures salespeople? It was said that this shrewd business owner only made appointments in the late afternoon when the sun sat behind his desk. That bright, burning light would sit behind his head like he was some angelic figure from a Renaissance painting.

So, of course, he was also the guy who nobody could sell. And it was Kevin's turn to try.

The rep walked into the 4:30 PM appointment, and there the man sat, sun at his command, resting on his right shoulder like a brilliant second head.

The salesman went right into the pitch, working his flip chart on the buyer's desk and sharing the financial impact of the company's insurance programs. The prospect listened intently, and Kevin had a glimmer of hope for a sale. His problem was that he'd also had a late night previously and a long workday before arriving. As the business owner asked a question, Kevin squeezed his eyes shut for one moment's rest from the radiant sunlight.

And promptly fell asleep.

He was awakened by a rough hand shaking his shoulder. The owner had walked around his desk and was sarcastically spouting, "Hey, if I'm keeping you awake, I can come back later."

His dark wit wasn't funny to the rep either. Kevin was humiliated and backed out of his office, apologizing profusely. The buyer dramatically ended the failed appointment by slamming the door in the salesman's face.

Postmortem: Whoa Kevin! Instead of rambling reps boring buyers, we have a seller who puts himself to sleep. If you look at your career like you are a professional athlete in the sport of financial services, you'll take better care of yourself physically (health and appearance) as well as mentally (closing strategies) and socially (rapport-building skills). Buyers respect sellers in good physical condition who exude—at the proper times—calm confidence and great energy. Invest in rest. Buyers will be glad that your appearance is congruent with the game in which you compete. And you will eliminate one roadblock on the path to a new client relationship.

● ● ●

In the following horror story, a rep's first impression puts an immediate end to a potential client. How soon can you guess her mistake?

A Collision Course in Failure

In two decades of selling financial services, Amy experienced everything that could possibly happen on a sales call. She just never got flustered any longer when a surprise occurred. That was true—right up until this appointment.

After a couple of months of phone calls, she finally had a well-to-do prospect agree to let her sit down in his home to review his financial future. So, on a warm summer evening, the sales pro drove into a beautiful community of very large custom-built homes. She glanced at the directions, saw his street was next, and turned into a cul-de-sac.

As Amy glanced again at her directions to verify the house number, she felt something hit her car. Actually it was her car that hit the something. And that something was (by now) a very loudly screaming little girl.

She slammed the car into park and jumped out, heart racing, head dizzy with fear. This girl had ridden her tricycle down her driveway and into the side of the car. When Amy realized that the child wasn't really hurt, just frightened, the rep began to shake. That was a very close call.

And then it got just a bit worse. As a man and his wife ran out of their house and down the driveway, she noticed the house number behind them.

Amy had just hit her prospect's five-year-old daughter.

Her explanation meant nothing to the father. It might have been okay if he was simply angry or scared, but his eyes flashed pure hatred at the woman—this insurance pro who was going to take care of his health and wealth needs.

Amy was asked to leave and, of course, never got the man on the phone again. She summed up her experience like this, "I guess I showed my prospect that he did need insurance. He just had no intention of buying it from me."

Postmortem: Distractions are often a problem in business. They destroy our focus. In fact, multitasking is best left to computers. When we do two things at once, we usually do them both poorly. If Amy had kept her focus, she might have at least completed her appointment. Don't multitask. You can tell when someone is on the phone with you reading e-mail or similarly distracted. Don't do this to others or yourself. This is worse on the road. Reading a map and driving a car don't mix any better than drinking and driving.

● ● ●

We all have to constantly be aware of first impressions at networking programs—those after-hours business scenarios where we hunt for potential prospects. Those of us who show up for these networking events wonder if they will result in a magical moment with a mammoth-sized prospect. Sometimes it almost does . . .

Handing Hope Away on a
Business Card

Jillian was invited to a business reception and knew that a very important prospect would be there. She had targeted the man for a while and was anxious to meet him, and so she arranged to have a mutual acquaintance introduce them. She was looking forward to this event, and a bit nervous about meeting "Mr. Big," who was in a position to give her company a large contract.

Everything went well. She met "Mr. Big," chatted for a few minutes, and he agreed to meet with her at his office the following week. Jillian was highly optimistic about the chances of getting her foot in the door with this company. She was sure she had made a great first impression.

When the rep got home that evening, she emptied the pockets of her jacket. Going through the business cards collected, she froze, realizing that a particular card was missing from her pocket. She had been to a doctor's office earlier in the day, and had a card for a follow-up appointment for a "very specialized" kind of woman's medical exam. This card was now missing.

Jillian had handed it to "Mr. Big" instead of her own without realizing it.

Imagine the look on "Mr. Big's" face when he went through the business cards he received that night. As the card would have Jillian's name on it for the appointment, there was no chance he wouldn't know who gave him the card. Jillian never did hear from "Mr. Big." He didn't return her calls or e-mails, although she left several messages.

Postmortem: Jillian networked her way to no sale. While hers was a particularly embarrassing card to give away, probably most of us have given someone else's card away by mistake, usually toward the end of an event, when you have more of other people's cards in your bag than your own. Here's a tip: always keep them in separate compartments or card holders—don't mix them together. Jillian probably would have loved a second chance to make a first impression. But here's why prospects don't give mulligans or do-overs: Prospects are inundated with advertising messages, aggressive salespeople, and personal concerns. It is easier to eliminate a choice (that would be Jillian), than to give it a second chance. We all go through this sorting of choices daily—you don't like that color or that guy's voice or that woman's hairstyle. Making a decision actually relieves the brain of the pressure of thousands of these daily messages. You can distinguish yourself from those other cries for attention by attending to the details of how you first present yourself. MEMORABLE MAKES MONEY.

● ● ●

Some of the most amazing sales blunders paint a picture that is unbelievable . . .

No Pets Allowed

As David's team waited in the cool morning air, a pit bull came up to them and, from his bloody jowls, dropped a half-dead chicken he had stolen from his owner's coop. He'd obviously been chewing it for some time. Well, the chicken was mortally wounded and was making a horrific groaning noise.

What were they doing there? David had just made a significant sale by phone to install a heating and air-conditioning system in an upscale home that sat nicely on several acres of farmland just outside the city limits.

On the day their work was to begin, he accompanied his installation crew to meet the homeowner at the job site. They were to go over the proposed plans and get the contracts signed. The workers and David arrived at the house that morning a little early, and the man of the house had not yet arrived at the home from his place of business a few minutes away.

So this chicken was gurgling on the ground, and it became very apparent that someone had to put this poor creature out of its misery—and quickly! Grabbing a 2×4 wooden board from the work truck, David took the chicken and began ramming his head into the ground with the board—as hard as he could. All the while the sales rep is thinking, "I don't know if the ground was too soft or that chickens are incredibly resilient, but this chicken would not die!"

The harder he hit it with the board, the louder the chicken groaned. This went on for some time and was quite amusing to the crew, who were laughing as he pounded the bird into the ground again and again. In all the commotion, what they did not notice was the homeowner pulling up behind them in his truck. There was this group of guys in his driveway, laughing and carrying on, and beating one of his chickens to death with a 2×4!

After the guy's initial shock and a heartfelt explanation of the unfortunate circumstances, the homeowner eventually let David's workers begin the job.

Postmortem: This is too funny! David's story paints a vivid picture and points out something we do too often to undermine our selling efforts. We usually talk too much when we sell and in the same way we can act too much as well. David didn't have to do anything with the chicken and he would have been fine. But I'll bet he wouldn't have missed making that memory for anything. Also, we don't endorse animal sacrifice to appease the sales gods.

● ● ●

Sometimes our personal lives intersect with the professional. In this woman's story, that crossover backfires badly.

How to Unsell a Religious Organization

Linda walked into a big singles party and was greeted by the host, who, gesturing to a giant bowl of multicolored condoms, offered, "Grab a handful." That fistful of rubber was to lead to Linda's most embarrassing moment in sales.

Senior seminars were proving so profitable that no financial services pro could ignore the potential. So Linda began to heavily promote herself in her community. She set up, publicized, and presented to seniors of all ages. Her personal strategy was to go through churches. Many of them had ministries or services that focused on their growing elderly population.

The Catholic retirement home was, therefore, a great fit for a group that needed her help. A few phone calls got the rep to the priest who managed the property. He accepted Linda's offer to discuss this over lunch.

She selected the best restaurant in town. "Father Prospect" showed up with his assistant for the meal. As they ate, Linda gave her pitch to do his senior presentation.

Conversation went great, and there was a high level of interest.

Linda reached into her wallet to pay the check, whipped out her American Express Gold card, and a condom flew across the table and landed in the priest's plate of food!

The woman was mortified! She remembers the moment too well, "The instant replay of that scene continues to video across my mind. How memorable is that impression for a conservative Catholic? Young single gal wants to help her community. Hopefully it's okay that she carries condoms with her to lunch. Oops! I wouldn't be giving birth to any new business today."

Postmortem: While Linda might not lament her liberal lifestyle, she probably now realizes it needn't be revealed to everyone. First be professional, rather than personal, with prospects. This can help them be comfortable with you, your organization, and, mostly, your product. Like a sales call, a fine meal sells itself first in its presentation on the plate. You should focus on doing the same.

● ● ●

Did you ever dream about a brilliant idea that would make you an instant millionaire? In this story, our inventor would have been better off playing the lottery . . .

New Invention Gets Off the Ground—Briefly

Barry's company was selling a new invention to the housewares market: a unique axe. This tool was designed so that when a user struck wood, the force was dispersed into the axe head and less force ran up the owner's arms. If you chopped a lot of wood for a fireplace or wood stove (as in rural areas), this product was a big stress reliever from the agony of daily wood-chopping chores.

Barry managed to secure an appointment with the buyer of a national hardware chain and shared the story of the axe with him. He was immediately intrigued. The man lived in a beautiful home in the mountains and cut his own wood! So Barry gave his big-bucks prospect the prototype to try out.

The buyer went home after work, carried the axe out his back door, laid a log on his chopping block, and swung.

The axe head flew off the handle and disappeared through his kitchen window.

The shocked and unsold buyer called the following morning to tell Barry he would not incur the liability to his tens of thousands of customers by selling such a dangerous product.

Their new product died a fairly quiet death.

Postmortem: Barry's hope for a national contract is cut down when he prematurely took his product to market. Now if he ever did fix the problem, it's unlikely that this key buyer would still consider carrying the axe in hundreds of hardware stores. There are two lessons here.

First, represent a quality product. A quality product labels you as a quality business professional. You can peel off that label by selling poorly, but handling an item or service of quality is a huge advantage in sales.

The second lesson is the old concern about first impressions. Barry had his shot at 15 minutes of fame. He only left a bad feeling of suspicion with the buyer after the flying axe show. Barry now has lots of work ahead to regain credibility so that he can introduce other product lines to the buyer. Protect your reputation and your one shot because appointments at this level are precious since they're hard to land.

● ● ●

In making good first impressions, insulting a prospect is rarely a useful strategy. This rookie rep's flippant comment makes her first impression also her last.

Rookie Runs Off at the Mouth

Dick had been training a rookie rep, a gal with no prior sales experience. And finally he felt she was ready to make her first sales presentation and make both of them some money. This prospect was Dick's own existing client who was looking to replace some badly dated equipment.

The decision makers came into the demonstration area for the presentation when disaster struck. The rookie salesgal told the client's vice president of office services, "The new equipment is so easy to operate your grandchildren could do it blindfolded."

The VP promptly told her in a voice that could have frozen ice that "My oldest child is 15 and she'd better not be pregnant with my grandchild."

The visitors cut the demo short, saying they weren't that impressed with what they saw and left the premises.

Dick was shocked at how quickly a hot prospect had chilled to the sale. He sat down with the new rep to debrief her on what he felt went right with her presentation and what needed work on for the future. The young woman told her manager that the woman VP looked so old she had to be a grandmother (the woman was only 39; the salesgal was 23). Dick told the rookie, as politely as possible, that assumptions were the mother of all screwups and father to lost sales. He reinforced that wisdom with some more, offering one of his training credos: "God gave all of us two eyes, two ears, and one mouth. Don't try to make up for the deficiency by doubling your talking efforts."

Postmortem: Too many lost sales are the result of salespeople who talk themselves "out" of the close. Before I founded Sales Autopsy, I was managing a rep who would not shut up. She kept pitching, even after the prospect said yes. I kicked her in the ankle under the table, and she let out this strange squawk. It confused the man sitting opposite us and tore my rep's nylons, but we got the sale. You want to get the prospects talking with a leading question like, "Well, thanks for coming to the demonstration. You must be busy. What concern is serious enough that you would take time from your workday, drive here, and look at our equipment?" You won't find out what the real problem is (the prospect isn't going to share that yet), but you'll be on track. Now, just keep asking things like, "Tell me more" and "Is that really that bad?" You talk a little. They talk a lot. You find out what business you're really in—solving problems that affect more than the person across from you. Learn to dig deeply with brief questions; you'll get prospects to express their real frustrations, and they'll love you when you rid them of the things that make them anxious.

● ● ●

In this tale, a salesman thinks he's already "in" with his customer. He learned that we all need to keep making good first impressions with everyone else that customer employs . . .

Customer on the Warpath

A few years back, while working for a midsized distributor of specialty beers, Dan experienced an incident that taught him a dramatic lesson and has made him especially careful of language choices, and conscious of whom he was speaking to.

One day, his sales route took him to a casino, a very good, high-volume account. As it happens, a Native American tribe operated this casino, and many of the employees and managers were, of course, members of that tribe. From having worked with them for a year, Dan was very comfortable with this account: He knew all the protocols, security checks, and rules, so the beer rep serviced them in a friendly, confident manner.

As Dan entered an area to access the cooler and take inventory, the security guard who was normally there was not—and a woman stood guard over the entrance. The first words out of his mouth were the ones that had become his standard greeting to *all* clients Dan felt comfortable with.

"How's it goin,' Chief?" he said, and stepped into the walk-in cooler.

Those four simple words meant the death of Dan's services to that account. As he exited the cooler, an obviously perturbed woman intercepted him and said, "Some of the people who work here would probably be offended by what you just said, mister!"

Dan recalls, "At first I missed the meaning. Then the connection between calling her 'Chief' and this being an Indian casino hit me. My face immediately turned a brilliant shade of red! I'd never done anything so dumb before. Shaken, I stuttered an attempt at a most sincere apology, pleading for forgiveness."

It was too late; Dan was asked, nicely, to leave.

Back at the office, his sales manager had already taken a phone call from the customer, "If your company wishes to continue to do business with us, that racist salesman is not to enter the premises!"

Dan lost the account to another rep.

Postmortem: How would you like to be Dan's sales manager, taking that phone call from an angry client? Here's how a good coach would handle Dan: First, Dan already knows he blew the call, so there's no need to beat him up further. You would teach him that when it comes to social procedure, business is business. Never allow yourself to become complacent just because you feel you "know" your client! Watch and think carefully about your choice of words, especially any words that sound insincere. Is "How's it going?" a sincere greeting? Most of the time, it's not. Say something meaningful, like "I love coming to your property," then explain why. And, please, use the individual's name. It's your best bet to really connect with them.

● ● ●

In the following story, a strange, supersized meal mishap ends a relationship right at the beginning . . .

Memorable Lunch, Missed Sale

Jeff and another employee flew in from California for a lunch meeting with two conservative Midwest grocery executives. They were interested in developing the relationship and making use of Jeff's research services. The consultant who accompanied Jeff was there to provide technical expertise.

They picked up the clients and went to their favorite restaurant, a really chic downtown place. It was a rehabbed loft with funky furnishings, neon lights, and a wild menu. After being seated, Jeff excused himself to visit the men's room, which was just as wild as the rest of the place. The sink was a fountainlike structure in the middle of the room, with floor pedals to turn on the water. Paper towels hung from the ceiling.

After returning to the table, the consultant went to the men's room. Then the clients got up to go. The clients returned quickly, red-faced and laughing. The consultant came back and a normal business lunch followed, with talk about some upcoming projects they wanted bids on. Jeff and his partner dropped them off at their office, then flew home.

When he called the clients the next day to get their feedback on the meeting, they told Jeff that it went well, but they felt "your buddy was a little weird." When he asked them to elaborate, they said, "Well, we walked into the men's room and he was standing on his tiptoes, peeing into the sink!" Jeff couldn't control his laughter at the image it painted and told them that the offbeat furnishings were probably a bit confusing.

Postmortem: Well, the execs never did engage Jeff's firm in any studies, and to this day he thought that they felt these two sales guys were a couple of strange dudes from California. Jeff has two issues to deal with here. First, after hearing the problem, don't be afraid to ask a question like this: "Wow, you probably have some concerns about doing business with someone like that, don't you?" It takes guts, but it can deflate the balloon of doubt floating overhead. Get the issues on the table. Conservative buyers still do business with West Coast weirdos—if they need what you've got. Second, there's a great deal of energy invested in sales lunches. Think hard about doing these meals. Are they a good time investment? The conversation might be more focused at your office or the prospect's, where time is more highly valued and respected. Save lunches for that rare close, or better yet, for a celebration to thank new clients for their wisdom in selecting you.

● ● ●

Crash on Contact • Wrap-Up

Before we get into a fantastic first impression strategy, let's just quickly cover some of the reasons salespeople ruin their initial interaction with prospects. The first few tales were about conditioning—staying in shape. Then we had a couple of stories about reps who couldn't seem to come across in a professional fashion. We also had some unexpected events that reared up and bit the sales reps in the wallet. The fact is, you are going to get in shape and it will be evident, or you just won't care about improving that area. You'll be surprised by occurrences you didn't want or plan on happening, and you'll learn to handle those as you grow (more tips and tales on this topic in the next chapter). Your biggest concern as you first interact with a stranger, be it the smallest or largest of sales calls, should be to get and stay focused.

I'll give you a tool today that will give you focus at the start of every contact. It will keep you from being intimidated by prospects who bully you. It will keep you from "winging it" when kicking off your call. You will close more business. This strategy is a true, world-class selling secret. With this you can solve a majority of first impression problems and come across as a true professional in the art and skill of sales.

In psychology, a critical concept used in helping change occur with patients is called "behavioral contracting." This means the counselor asks the person seeking help to agree to the following: (1) the purpose of the meeting (today and a commitment to the next steps); (2) how much time will be committed; and (3) open, honest communication between both parties.

The best sales professionals apply this thinking in all of their dialogues with prospects.

In 20+ years of selling, managing, and training reps, this is BY FAR the best idea I've ever heard. It is actually built into the selling system used by 180 offices of the Sandler Sales Institute (*www.sandler.com*).

There are two ways you can initiate contact: face-to-face and by phone. (No, online is not the third method—garnishing someone's attention through e-mail is virtually fruitless. In fact e-mail marketing makes cold calling look like a trip to the bank.)

In every meeting (by phone or in person), you essentially will say,

"Mr./Ms. Prospect, you said on the phone that we'd have 45 minutes together. Is that still good? Great. And is it okay for us to set an objective and outcome for this time? Let's do this. You'll want some questions answered and I will, too. So let's just be candid with one another, and if it looks like what you and I are trying to accomplish are just not in synch with one another, will you please tell me that this doesn't seem like a fit? And if I realize that I can't help you, I'll tell you right away, as your time is precious. Okay? Please, don't worry about hurting my feelings. Just be honest, so I don't get the wrong signal and hound your e-mail and voice mail while you try to figure out a way to ignore me. Now, what's the biggest concern you wanted to address during our time today?"

And we're off and running. And guess who's about to do most of the talking? The prospect, of course—which is just how the sales gods wanted us to live our lives.

When I was both selling sales training and training salespeople, I required all reps to print out a copy of their behavioral contract and keep it with them. They could review it just prior to a call. And by sharing their document with others who sell, each rep could find better wording and keep the other accountable by using this tool. But the best part is it structures your sales appointments and keeps your selling on track. This is just too valuable a tool to ignore.

Now, here's the fun part. If these prospects don't want to play the game by your rules, you take your ball (or your briefcase) and go home.

Isn't this another way of disqualifying prospects? Why would you want to invest time with someone who won't be honest or respect your time, now and in the future (when they refuse to set a next step)? Agreeing on how the meeting is to progress is the sign of the ultimate professional.

It will send you into the world-class category—that of the elite sales pro.

You can end first impression mistakes today! Put into play the strategies you just learned.

Fix your first impressions by establishing a behavioral contract at the start of every call. It's good psychology and great selling! Sit down with someone who sells, share this concept, and work with them to design your own "contract." Remember to identify

- how much time is committed to the call;

- what the outcomes, goals, or focus of the conversation is;

- how both parties will offer honest feedback; and

- how to set next steps.

Get this critical piece of the selling puzzle completed today, and you will give your prospects fantastic first impressions.

CHAPTER SIX

Combat Pay

Adversity over Products, Prospects, and Animals

The 10 Most Common Causes of Accidental Death in the United States

	CAUSE	TOTAL	%
1.	Motor vehicle	42,271	42.1
2.	Fall	14,992	14.9
3.	Poisoning	14,053	14.0
4.	Suffocation	4,941	4.9
5.	Burning	3,370	3.4
6.	Drowning	3,179	3.2
7.	Transportation (excluding motor vehicles	2,799	2.8
8.	Natural/environmental	1,387	1.4
9.	Pedestrian	1,236	1.2
10.	Striking by/against object	890	.9
	Total accidental deaths	100,441	100%

Source: National Center for Injury Prevention and Control (U.S. Government)

Hey, selling is not on this list! People don't die from sales work. In 25 years of selling, I've never had a colleague drown, suffocate, or get poisoned on the job.

There are times, however, when we really do earn combat pay.

A lot of selling is about good times and tough. When I think of a sales pro's experience, a metaphor comes to mind—hail. Do you know where hail comes from?

Hail or ice pellets are born in the clouds of a thunderstorm. Strong gusts of wind toss raindrops upward to freezing heights again and again. Each time they grow in size until they are heavy enough to fall to earth. If you would cut and count the onionlike layers in a hailstone, they would tell you how many times it has been tossed up into freezing altitudes and down again. White layers are added up high—as ice crystals; clear layers are added in the lower, warmer regions of the cloud. If we cut into your experience as a sales professional, we'd find lots of layers: times you spent in freezing cold conditions with rough prospects, and warmer times when you enjoyed the recognition of your successes from peers, family, and your bank.

Be encouraged; be tough. Whether dodging hail or staplers, the sun will soon shine on your efforts. And you will safely and successfully emerge from your time on the sales battlefield.

Sales horror stories related to various forms of adversity provide more entertainment than any other category in my collection. Enjoy the offbeat, unexpected, and outrageous situations our reps find themselves in as we wade through the worst of bad reps, bad prospects, and simple bad luck.

Hold Your Breath, Close Your Eyes, and Sell

The sales rep is standing in a London morgue, and the doctor is doing what doctors do in morgues.

How did Jason get there? It was his first job selling for an American company in the United Kingdom. The company supplies a variety of voice-recording equipment to businesses. So he's normally pitching handheld devices to lawyers or call-logging products for stockbrokers. Then his firm introduced a new device that allows people to operate the equipment with a waterproof foot control.

In a meeting with a customer in a hospital, Jason mentions this new equipment. The executive sits up in his seat and says this is perfect for a colleague. Cool, a referral. He then picks up the phone and arranges a meeting that afternoon. Very cool, a referral with a happy ending in sight, a close.

This is going to be a breeze, so Jason ducks out for a hearty lunch (celebrating a bit prematurely), then heads back to meet his new customer. The physician is very interested and asks if he could set up for a demonstration and a trial use. With a spring in his step, the rep heads to his car and grabs the equipment. He's shown to the room where the demo is to occur—it's the morgue.

Jason suspends the microphone from a lighting boom overhead and places the foot control below the examination table.

At this point he's still expecting a "dry" run. But Jason was just not that fortunate.

The prospect walks in wearing surgical greens, closely followed by his assistant and a porter pushing a body on a gurney. Jason flies through a two-minute run-down of how to operate the equipment, and the doctor then (gulp) asks the rep to stay while he gets the hang of it. Jason is thinking, I know I can cope with anything; I'm adaptable. No worries, I can handle this.

The sheet is drawn back, and the doctor starts his work. No way is Jason watching this! He finds a point on the wall to fix his eyes and begins to answer questions. As Jason relaxes a little, the physician asks something about how waterproof the foot control was and if it would stand up to hosing down. The already skittish sales rep turns to answer and catches a full view of the body, with internal organs sitting neatly atop and around an exposed cavity.

The words for the answer never made it out of Jason's mouth, but his lunch did.

He later managed to close the sale, although he couldn't credit his sales technique. His company was the only supplier of this type of equipment.

___**Postmortem:** Jason! Launching himself and his lunch into his new sales career! Anxiety related to unexpected circumstances can be a killer on a call. Jason had a hint for anyone else selling in hospitals: Dress for success—but don't wear your best suit in a morgue, the smell never quite disappears. As you progress in selling, you will encounter diversity in prospects and personalities that will astound you. The most you can plan for is to "expect the unexpected." Much of this book is meant to help you develop the mental flexibility to deal with things that aren't going smoothly.

● ● ●

Adversity shows up in many forms. In the next two tales, both from the same industry, one rep encounters equipment failure while another encounters a jealous spouse.

Sandblasting the Finish Off a Sales Career

In a previous sales life Tim spent a summer selling vacuum cleaners—that is, home-cleaning systems.

He had been doing a lot of demonstrations and failed to stop and properly check the equipment. As a result, Tim didn't notice the tear in the vacuum cleaner bag (you can see what's coming, but the rep didn't and neither did the homeowners).

The sales tactic in this business was to show people how powerful the vacuum cleaner was by dumping a full pound of sand onto their carpet and then easily cleaning it up with the vacuum.

Tim piled up the sand and hit that power switch. The sand took a different route than normal. It went shooting through the vacuum, into the bag, through the tear in the bag, and out the back of the vacuum!

It happened very quickly, and Tim didn't even know something was wrong until the screaming and laughing. He swung around and saw that he was sandblasting a whole family of onlookers in their own living room.

Tim's lesson is in his words, "The moral of the story is to make sure your equipment is top-notch before you go on to make a fool of yourself. Abe Lincoln once said that if he had eight hours to chop down a tree, he would spend the first six hours sharpening the blade."

Postmortem: So Tim's sale dies in a desert of his own creation. He nailed it with his analysis of what went wrong with product sales: You live or die with your equipment. This is why a soldier is taught to dismantle his weapon blindfolded, so he can do it in the dark when danger looms near. Your equipment includes your vehicle, which can break down and break appointments. Or it might look bad and send a message that you're not successful. Care for your car, computer, and anything that helps carry you to the close. Again, you'll avoid surprises that keep you from commission checks.

● ● ●

As promised, another vacuum tale . . .

Door-to-Door to Bedroom to Car

Ron was selling vacuum cleaners in his early, dummy days of selling. And he was so thankful that he had graduated away from working door-to-door. But he remembers a woman who asked him to come in one morning and show her how powerful these cleaners were.

His sales tactic was to offer big proof of the vacuum's power by putting a filter on it and cleaning the bedsheets. Stuff you could not see showed up in the most disgusting dark colors on the filter—dead skin, dust mites, and more. If Ron could vacuum the bed, he could close the sale. It was that simple.

He plugged into the wall and was just moving back the bedding when a man walked into the bedroom. Ron recalled, "He was huge, like three or four times bigger than me!"

"Who is this?" The man barked. His neck began getting red, the color running up through his cheeks and into his angry eyes. Did Ron mention that he was really, really big?

"Oh, honey." Was all the salesman heard and he bolted. He only had the handle of the cleaner in his hand as he blasted past the guy and down the stairs—didn't even unplug the thing. The whole unit came bouncing down after Ron. He was out the door and in his car, pulling away while still pulling the vacuum into his lap, door open, heart hammering, sweat sweating.

The terrified sales rep squealed down the street, equipment trailing out the driver's door.

The rest of the sales team thought his experience was hysterical. And as if embarrassment and a lost sale weren't costly enough, Ron had to pay for the vacuum cleaner that got dragged behind his car.

Postmortem: A rep running like a rabbit. There's a picture for you. A sales career is full of those experiences we look back on and say, "If I'd handled that differently, could I have still closed it?" What would you do in Ron's place? The ability to instantly assess a situation and respond is what keeps soldiers alive in battle. Yeah, I would have run, too.

● ● ●

Staying with the theme of equipment ruining commissions, in this story, a rep makes a lasting impression by "presenting" to more people than she'd intended . . .

Smoldering Customer Fires
Saleswoman

Marie sells a line of welding products and alloys, and part of the sales process entails doing demonstrations to show the customers how well the product works. She was working on a relatively new customer and had just done a seminar on Cutting and Torch Safety.

Now she was back again, trying to move the company from a couple of small test orders to a real, life-sized client. Today's demonstration was for a new type of oxygen cutting lance. Marie had all the key guys around for the demo, and they chose a huge piece of steel for her to cut through. She took out one rod and started blasting through the material. The demo was going great. However, a small fire started on the floor from some smoldering metallic debris and burning sawdust. It got a bit smoky, but the problem was quickly smothered.

As she showed off her hot, new equipment, the maintenance man got a phone call. Marie heard him say, "We're just doing some cutting in the maintenance department." The demo was finally completed. Everyone was suitably impressed. So Marie wrote up the quote for the supervisor and began packing to leave the plant. It looked like this little customer was growing up after all.

As she was checking out with the security guard, he advised Marie that she had "caused quite a commotion in there." What specifically did that mean? He said that the smoke from the maintenance department had come up through the mailroom ventilation system and into the office, evacuating the entire building!

This would not have been too bad, but there was a big corporate meeting that day, and Marie's demo fiasco had also evacuated the president, chairman/CEO, treasurer, and several vice presidents.

At the time the guard was telling her this, he was laughing. And frankly it was pretty funny, so both Marie and her district manager laughed about it hysterically as they walked to the parking lot.

It wasn't funny after that. The maintenance supervisor still has not returned her calls, so needless to say, she didn't get the order! Marie has had no business from the company since then. You might say she was "fired" for burning her customer.

   Postmortem: Poor Marie—lost her baby customer before it could grow up to be a healthy adult client. Marie was doing all the right things, right up to the end. But looking at the story from a different angle, I do like how she nurtured this client by gaining a few small orders, hoping to land that big sale. Are you struggling with prospects who could possibly be huge customers? Find a way to offer them some small sale. This changes your status from an adversarial, hard-pitching salesperson to a strategic partner and vendor. This switch in perception gives you ongoing access to your buyers. You will find them less likely to hide behind voice mail. Even the buyer's assistant will treat you differently. Land that little sale, and begin building a foundation for success with your big potential clients.

●　●　●

This next tale proves that man's best friend is not necessarily a rep's . . .

Cold, Wet Calling

Wayne, a financial services rep, was making some rural farm-to-farm calls for his brokerage firm. He'd drive miles and miles through a farm area, pull onto properties, and introduce himself. Of course, these were all cold calls, so he experienced the complete range of responses:

- Invitations to come in for coffee

- People at home who wouldn't answer the door for a stranger

- Doors slammed in his face

- Shotguns gesturing him back to his car

Today was a one-in-a-million experience. It would provide a teaching moment for all the salespeople Wayne would manage—in the years to follow.

The large, well-weathered face of a farmer peered through the screen door on his porch. Wayne introduced himself and the company, and the man began laughing. Did he have a bad experience with the firm in the past? The rep had certainly said nothing humorous. Wayne began asking some introductory financial questions in order to determine the prospect's level of investment interests.

He kept laughing. It was one of those gut laughs that meant he was enjoying himself, body and soul. What was so amusing? What entertainment was a cold-calling, door-to-door salesman providing?

Then it hit him—literally. Wayne finally felt something and looked down. The farmer's dog had come up the porch behind him. A hind leg was hiked and the filthy animal was, well he was writing in yellow ink all over Wayne's pants.

This call was over. Embarrassed, Wayne left with his proverbial tail between the legs.

Postmortem: That would be, in my mind, the ultimate rejection. And maybe our agriculture sales friends should be sporting rubber socks and packing cattle prods. Wayne's lesson is a simple one. Keep the faith and keep selling. Cold calling can be tough, but probably the worst that can happen is a dog marking his territory on your pants. Unless, of course, you've had a prospect do that. I'll want to hear that story today!

● ● ●

And another dog intercepts a sale . . .

Unexpectedly Ugly Upselling Event

Jim took a young woman agent, new to the insurance business, out on a call. Seventeen years' experience in selling life insurance and investment products has developed him into a resource for his manager. This means that occasionally he'd be asked to take a rookie out to observe the old pro at work in front of clients.

This call was to upsell a business owner to bigger things. Jim had a little business from this man, but was now going to attempt to take over his company's 401(k) plan investments.

Jim cautioned his protégé that this was a good, solid guy with a good, solid business, but his office would be a mess; it was a dirty manufacturing environment. And don't be surprised to see cats and a dog running around in the squalor.

When they arrived, the client moved several piles of papers off the two chairs in front of his desk, and the rep and his trainee sat down and began discussing how Jim's client could enhance the performance of his stock plan.

As the experienced salesman moved toward a close, a strange smell began to hover in the room. At first, he thought that his rookie friend had passed gas or that perhaps the client had. Then Jim realized that the owner's Doberman had done what doggies do—left a big steaming pile right between the chairs Jim and the woman occupied in front of the client's desk.

Everyone was horribly embarrassed, and the two of them quickly left without closing the deal.

But Jim's assessment of the ending is classic: "The tough part was that I might still have closed the guy—doggie doo and all—if my partner hadn't started gagging."

Postmortem: Well, that memory is burned into Jim's brain, eyes, and nose. One of the biggest differences between experienced and rookie sales professionals is the ability to handle the unexpected. Jim knew that he could still stay on track to upsell this client. However, his rookie ride-along couldn't keep from physically reacting to an awful, awkward situation. Here are two suggestions for handling embarrassing scenes (you will not like this first idea): First, Jim could have begun to clean up the mess (or offered to). If he had, how could the client have refused to work with him?! Second, Jim could have made a joke about the situation, downplaying it as a minor disruption, then returned to the conversation. Don't be afraid of taking some risk when you sell. Often, sales professionals with more guts will prevail. Don't let an awkward occurrence drain the life out of your sales call. Address it, then move on. To handle the unexpected, simply stay completely focused on your goal for that meeting.

● ● ●

As if we haven't had enough animals complicating the lives of reps, a cow makes its contribution to a dramatic international sales horror story . . .

Disappearing Client, Hiding or Dead?

When Brandy landed the life policy on a hotshot entrepreneur, it was a huge boost to her selling career. The $5 million policy was great for Brandy's bank account. It was even better for her credibility in the office. In an industry in which women are selling in much smaller numbers than men, it was nice to see her reputation on the rise.

Shortly after he passed his medical exams and was approved for coverage, the entrepreneur began to struggle with his business. While on an unexplained trip to eastern Europe, he was killed in a bizarre plane accident. As he was walking across a runway, he was sucked into an engine of the jet he was about to board.

Brandy's firm was concerned about verifying the death in order to pay on the claim. The trouble is, unlike the United States, many countries don't issue death certificates. So the insurance company had to hire investigators who flew across the world to interview "witnesses" to the awful scene. Some of their stories didn't quite match.

The final fishy clue proved the whole incident was a fraud perpetrated by the near-bankrupt businessman.

The blood on the plane's engine belonged to a cow.

That guy still hasn't arrived back in the United States. Prison is probably much worse than bankruptcy.

And Brandy's growing reputation has been temporarily arrested, while she listens to mumbled "moos" behind her back at the office.

Postmortem: This is a terrible story (and a bit funny). How can you turn this disaster into a positive experience? Well, the marketer in me got really fired up when I heard it. Brandy could jump-start a promotional campaign for her business by speaking to companies and clubs around her working market territory. If her company would allow her to share this tale (some details must be left out), what group wouldn't love to hear a speaker with such a fascinating story? For Brandy herself, it's a lesson in how unpredictable life can be. Again, the sooner we learn to just shake our heads and move on, the healthier our heads are for selling.

● ● ●

Sometimes the sales life can be downright danger-ous—especially if the prospect is better armed than you . . .

Selling Knives and Firing Guns

Selling in the homes of consumers can be tricky and sometimes scary.

When Dave was a college student selling Cutco knives, a young lady locked him in her bedroom because her ex-boyfriend was kicking down the door, jealous that she was with a man. (At 19, Dave hardly qualified for the "man" label.) But at least a solid oak door separated him from harm's way, although it did concern the young rep that his knives were on the other side of the door.

Today, Dave is a bit better at selling, though still a college student and still a fairly new student of Cutco persuasion skills. He is learning both how tough and enjoyable sales can be—much more money and fun than, say, working in the school cafeteria.

So on a very cold, snowy night he called on a young married couple in a depressed area of Lowell, Massachu-setts. It's a classic picture of a home-based sales call. They were sitting at the kitchen table. At his right, in a high chair, sat a cute baby girl. Husband and wife, Axel and Judy, bracketed Dave on either end of the table.

The call was going along just fine and friendly—until Judy began to get very excited about the cutlery. Axel evidently imagined some big bucks flying from his pocket to Dave's and went on the attack.

He started insulting the rep and his wife as well. Axel said this guy sitting here was a slick salesman and threatened Judy with bodily harm if she bought even a potato peeler from him.

Dave was thinking he wished he were a slick salesman. He was also thinking that he'd witnessed his share of family fights, but this situation was much more animated and hostile than a normal argument over whether to spend a lot of money on kitchenware.

As Axel was raising his fist to Judy, the white knight in Dave decided to suit up and say, "Axel, Judy seems to like these knives, and she's the one who spends most of the day in the kitchen."

Next thing Dave saw was Axel pointing a very large gun, at his little girl! Just as he was about to pull the trigger, his arm swung toward the terrified rep, centered on his chest and BOOM! Dave flipped backwards off the chair, thinking he was dead. He staggered to his feet and scrambled for the door, leaving knives, coat, keys, and possessions behind. Diving through the apartment door, Dave heard Axel laughing.

Once out in the cold, the young man realized that he hadn't been shot and Axel was laughing because the blanks he fired at Dave have allowed him to get a free set of knives, and a perfectly sized winter coat.

<u>**Postmortem**</u>: A recurring theme in selling today is that prospects are better armed. This real story proves that theory. I hope you also saw right where Dave turned into a real sales dummy. He challenged the thinking of this prospect by trying to play husband against wife. Speaking down to a potential customer can only give them flashbacks of mom and dad doing the same—that's not an objection-handling decision. We create problems of our own by our choice of language and tone of voice. Be sensitive to how as well as to what you say to people, and you'll be a better sales pro. Here's a bonus thought—do the same away from the job and you'll be a better friend and family member as well.

● ● ●

There's one last stupid sales mistake to wrap up this chapter, but let's cover this whole adversity thing in one thought: How quickly do you recover from trouble?

You've probably heard, "We'll laugh about this later." I want you to laugh about these situations right now. The faster you move on, the healthier you are in your sales life. It's as simple as that.

Great sales professionals handle trouble just like throwing a light switch. It's done, move on, deal with what's left in front of you.

You can do this. You can make a decision, right now, on how you will handle future sales encounters that put you into the Twilight Zone—whether that means unexpected or just weird. So, how quickly will you adjust or recover from trouble, bad news, bad prospects?

You've had to do this your whole life, from when you encountered trouble with kids and classmates growing up all the way to breaking up with someone to dealing with death in the family. In sales, you can't afford to mourn. Move on instead. Throw the switch.

● ● ●

Sam, in this story, is one of my favorite salespeople ever. He screwed up and adjusted immediately to continue doing what he loved to do—sell.

Does Your Dog Bite?

While running a sales program, I met this older gentleman, Sam. He had these gigantic, soda-bottle glasses, thickest lenses I'd ever seen. He was a great phone salesman. Here's how he became so good.

Sam's eyes had always been bad, and he used to sell encyclopedias door-to-door.

At one home a woman answered her door. Sam heard a sound, squinted at her feet, and said, "Oh! How cute, what kind of dog do you have?"

She snapped back, "That's my baby girl!" And slammed the door in his face.

Sam realized right there that he could no longer sell face-to-face—with or without his magnifying glasses. But there was nothing he'd rather do. So Sam went right back to his office and convinced his manager to let him work inside sales from that day forward. On the phone, Sam now only has to focus on the words, rather than with his eyes. And he has since become a superb sales rep.

Postmortem: Sam stopped looking for success and listened instead. He moved from a visual selling life, face-to-face, to a verbal life, selling by phone. Sam came to crossroads and decided he loved selling too much to quit. So he adjusted his job to keep his career on track down the path to selling success. What inspires you? Sam was inspired by a negative experience. Have you encountered limitations, and are they holding you back or driving you on to better things? This old guy brought a grin to my face and a smile to my heart when he turned a big negative into a bigger positive. Go and do the same.

● ● ●

Combat Pay • Wrap-Up

Here are some questions to determine how conflict affects your sales ability. Answer each, then score yourself from 1 to 10 (10 meaning you are great at dealing with the situation).

- How well do you handle adversity?

- Can you quickly adjust your response to trouble?

- Can you quickly recover from it?

- Can you quickly move on?

There's an old saying that embodies selling wisdom at its finest. You simply categorize every contact as YES, NO, NEXT:

- It's a sale or

- It's not.

- If it isn't, move on.

- YES, NO, NEXT

How quickly can you throw the switch?

CHAPTER SEVEN

Becoming an Angel

Three Investments for Sales Pros

I Just Knew There Was a Question I Forgot to Ask

Here's another story of my own—again from my early days of selling stupidly.

I had found the perfect candidate to place in a sales job. Jane had three things going for her. She was a star salesperson, she was extremely professional in appearance, and her husband pitched for the Boston Red Sox. If you can't start a good conversation trying to place this woman into a sales position, you don't deserve to be in selling.

The worst problem—my biggest objection—in the search business is that most companies won't pay headhunting fees for salespeople. They can run an ad in the paper and get hundreds of responses. So why spend thousands of dollars on my services?

This woman was worth the money and I knew it when I landed a decision maker on the phone. This magazine publisher was so excited about Jane that when he agreed to pay my fee if he hired her, I skipped asking about his business and closed him right then for her interview.

Jane was supposed to call me immediately after the meeting, but an excited magazine executive called me first, and spoke the words a recruiter lives to hear: "I love her. She's perfect for the job. I'll pay her asking salary." He added that she was great looking and that was a big bonus in his business.

I told him that I'd call him back—as soon as I found out how she felt about him.

Her call came.

"I can't believe you sent me there!" she screamed into the phone.

It was a pornography magazine.

I'd had no idea. The title of the publication didn't give a hint. No wonder the guy was raving about her looks. Who knows what kind of prospects she'd be calling on? Jane was very cool about it. We had some good laughs later, but it was nothing compared with the laughs in the Red Sox clubhouse when the story worked its way from her husband to the team.

Postmortem: Early in my selling career I had not yet invested myself in adapting a selling system to my business. So I had not yet learned to ask all the critical questions that were needed before offering a solution to the prospect's problem. What are the key inquiries you need to make early in each prospecting conversation? If I had asked what type of customer the magazine targeted, or requested a demographic description of its market, I would have discovered two things: (1) Jane might have immediately said no to the interview and (2) we could have targeted a salesperson who calls on that target market already, providing a perfect potential solution to that prospect's need. Today I'm a selling system evangelist. You can significantly improve earnings by putting some time and effort and possibly money into bettering your skills. While you're deciding how to do that, just start by creating a list of all the questions you should ask a prospect. Then get them answered before offering your solution.

● ● ●

In the world of entrepreneurs, venture capital, money, and investments, one solution to growth is to call on an angel. This is someone who provides individuals and organizations with the resources to skyrocket their performance. Angels help companies grow, expand, and provide upside in terms of great potential in earnings for those involved.

These stories will point to the ultimate angel who can send your earnings heavenward. That angel is you.

● ● ●

World-class sales professionals invest in themselves on a continual basis throughout their selling careers. In this story, a woman learns the hard way that a bargain is not an investment . . .

Sales Call Rained Out

Laura is from St. Louis and she's not vain, but she just feels that the Southern girl skin that covers her body is just too light (well, white) during summer months. To appear fit and healthy on all her sales calls, she would use tanning cream, or what the ladies call "bronzer." You know the stuff: Your friends get a kick out of it when you show up one day with two weeks' worth of sun on your face.

Laura's trip to the drugstore had led her to believe that this lotion must be really valuable because it was really expensive. At least most of it was. So Laura selected the cheapest tube on the shelf and began wearing it. And she felt great. That mental boost that can really change your attitude on sales calls was completely enhanced by Laura's magic lotion. She was confident, looking and acting like a successful professional when in front of prospects.

And then, like the weather, her luck changed.

She started the summer day with a tan blouse, white skirt and white pumps—a new outfit that showed off her new skin color quite well. The appointment was downtown, and she had to walk a couple blocks from her parking space, just as a rare summer shower started.

Briefcase over her head, Laura sprinted into the building and walked to the elevator, her big smile countering the big smiles that greeted her.

"Are you okay?" the receptionist asked as Laura found the office. She said she was just a bit rained on, but ready to go. Laura was led into a full boardroom.

As she strode up to the president he also said, "Are you okay?" That was strange. Then he pulled a linen handkerchief out of his pocket and handed it to the rep. She's thinking, "Who uses these anymore?" as she wiped the rain from her face . . .

And stared at a hanky, brown with her fake tan. Her eyes moved south as she looked down at a blouse and skirt and shoes, all streaked brown. Now she realized how silly her face must appear, equally streaked, since she just smeared her tan all over a gentleman's handkerchief.

In an instant that mental boost blew out of the room, leaving Laura feeling silly and incompetent. That presentation was pretty bad. Okay, it was horrible. And kind of gross. It was no sale.

Postmortem: You might realize from Laura's trouble that an investment in yourself should be a quality purchase. If she'd bought a better brand of tanning cream, she would still today be confident, happier, and darker. If you begin to see personal purchases as investments (just as your customers should see their purchases from you!), you'll change how you buy. What you wear and drive are considered reflections of you. Choose quality over cheap; you'll never regret it.

● ● ●

Proper personal care is one area of focus if you want to establish a deposit in your sales future. Bill is one of the America's top sales trainers. This vivid memory throws him back to his early days on the road . . .

Dress Down for Success

As a rookie rep Bill was extremely proud to land an appointment with an executive at a very large company. The young salesman flew into Indianapolis and spent the night relaxing in front of cable TV at his hotel.

After showering and putting on his new "selling" suit, Bill burrowed through the suitcase for his dress shoes. He dug some more, then frantically began clawing into clothes, hoping for a handful of stiff leather and laces. Nothing, they'd been left at home.

Next to the bed sat Bill's bright, white, high-top tennis shoes. It was all he had to cover his dress socks. Bill was thinking, "This executive is going to think that I am my company's village idiot."

Then the rookie began to get just plain nervous about everything. He started to sweat in his suit. A long look in the mirror, starting high and going down—the direction Bill's spirit was headed—revealed a young salesman with anxious eyes, a beautiful suit, and the latest Converse fashion statement.

Time to go. A quick shot of hair spray and he bolted for the elevator. The woman riding with him sniffed loudly and that's when the smell hit Bill as well: It was not hairspray coating his hair. It was Right Guard deodorant.

The introduction to the buyer became a study in non-verbal gestures. His right eyebrow lifted as he glanced at the shoes. His nose wrinkled when Bill leaned in to shake his hand. And his lips tightened as Bill began his presentation. The rep was so distracted and preoccupied by his personal blunders that his sales performance was miserable.

It was no sale of course. Why buy from an amateur? But Bill had time for one final humiliation as he left the building.

The elevator stopped on the first floor and opened up to waiting employees. Six pair of eyes flicked down to the young man's waist. His zipper was broken. It was up and open. And he didn't even have time to change before his return flight.

    Postmortem: Bill learned a most memorable lesson about anticipating potential problems and addressing them ahead of time. Have you ever spilled coffee or spaghetti on your clothes during a workday? How easy is it to put a spare shirt or blouse and some slacks or a skirt in your trunk? Bill now always has a complete change of clothing when he is out on calls. His spare garments are with him whether he is on a local appointment or away from home. The day you use those items, you'll be *so* grateful you anticipated trouble and it did not defeat you. Pack a spare outfit with your spare tire, starting tomorrow.

● ● ●

Aside from our personal care, the tools we use are reflections of who we are and how we present quality to our prospects and customers.

As my sales horror story collection grew, I began to notice a trend toward the wisdom in investing in one's business, and therefore one's future. So I started to stop paying the least I could for everything and instead went for quality and its twin brother longevity.

A funny incident branded my final moment of "see how much money I could save." I was at Circuit City buying a mouse for my laptop computer. Wow—$9.95 was a deal! I got it home and opened the package. A slip of paper fell out. It read, "Lead was used to produce this mouse. Please wash hands after using."

Are you kidding me? My mouse is built with a toxic substance and I should wash my hands every time I closed my computer?

Back I went to the store, where I showed a shocked manager what he was selling. The guy pulled all the product from the shelves and called corporate right then.

Who knows how many lives I saved?

After buying a better mouse, I continued my personal quality campaign by upgrading what I wear and what I drive. For example, quality shoes are a big deal when you spend lots of time on trade show floors. And my car? I just decided to make a serious investment increase in the vehicle I'm seen in and use to entertain. Managing your image is something you will find worth attending to.

Think and show quality and boost your sales image and earnings today. Shortly, you'll see that you'll want to invest in three areas of your life: clothing (appearance), tools, and education.

● ● ●

Next, in Fred's folly, he thinks his education is good enough—and pays for it by not getting paid . . .

Translation Travesty

Fred was doing training for one of the big national firms that have hundreds of events around the country. Each speaker/trainer was paid based on how well he or she performed in two ways: How well the attendees rated him or her, and how much product was sold in back of the room after the session. In fact, selling in the back made up a large portion of the trainer's income. And Fred was great at this. He was a hustler and sold loads of product. In fact, Fred did so well that he soon left to start his own speaking and training business—but not before having the pleasure of one royal disaster.

One day Fred's boss called him into the office because a client in Mexico City wanted one of the firm's classes taught. He wanted to know if Fred took the assignment, whether he would need an interpreter. Fred spoke good street Spanish. He had for years. So he said no, he could handle the training. The top trainer wasn't sharing money with anyone. A translator meant another person to split income with.

Do you know the difference between using passable Spanish and being able to communicate to a native Mexican business audience for an eight-hour seminar? Fred was about to learn.

At the first break half of the 100 attendees never returned.

After the second break half of the group left did not come back.

Fred was now down to 25 percent of the original audience to whom he hoped to sell product. But worst of all was the most unforgettable ending to the day. Before selling product, every trainer was taught to open the floor for questions. Today, only one gentleman raised his hand and in the most beautiful Spanish asked, "How do we get our money back?"

Fred sold nothing. People actually left handouts, workbooks, and flyers on the tables. He was a complete bust.

Fred swore that he would never put himself in an embarrassing business situation again.

Postmortem: Fred fumbles south of the border. This lesson is too easy. Stop being cheap. If you take shortcuts in your learning, it will ruin your earnings. Here is my advice that will help set your sights on making more money.

Go back to school.

Remember growing up how you'd be required to take a class and it just made no sense to you? Your friends would gather and grouse about it? "When are we ever going to use calculus in the real world?"

You can finally get learning under your belt and into your brain because that is exactly what you need for the real world of selling.

Even if your company will not provide the level of selling skills or coaching you need, you'll want to accept responsibility for your future and go get it yourself—even if it costs you more than you expect.

See, the best sales professionals are true investors in every aspect of their craft.

Everyone else is simply a tourist to the trade of selling.

I use the term *tourist* because of a speech I heard. Of his visit to the Vietnam War Memorial in Washington, D.C., a great speaker said, "Watching people at that wall, you could tell the difference between the tourists and 'investors.' The tourists are gawking and talking at this magnificent work of art. They show little outward regard for the seriousness and significance of this monument. The investors are quiet and respectful. Many are on their knees. The names on the wall signify the ultimate investment, made by comrades and loved ones giving their lives."

Someone who's invested in something has a different set of behaviors than a sightseer just passing through. And so this behavior reflects the attitude the salesperson has chosen. I've never met a tourist-mentality salesperson who was any good at his or her craft.

Don't be *casually committed* to your profession.
This is not about the company or product you represent, but your profession—SELLING! If your best is
70 percent, you're 30 percent short. And your earnings reflect that shortcoming.

● ● ●

Becoming an Angel • Wrap-Up

There are three ways to invest in yourself. You want
to invest in

1. *Personal appearance:* Your image sends a message.
   Can your clothing use an upgrade? How about
   your hairstyle or physical condition? If prospects
   have to live with looking at you, give them a
   pleasant and professional experience by way of
   your image.

2. *Tools:* This includes your car and computer,
   PDA, etc. Do you have any problems communi-
   cating with your office, prospects, or clients? Can
   you get information instantly, which is just how
   quickly it's expected today? Are you backing up
   your computer systems? Spend the money to
   avoid any aggravation that slows down your
   selling process as well as your ability to function

smoothly throughout the rest of your day. Buy the best. Just as you want to be the safest bet for prospects to buy from, you want your tool investments to be your safest selections in operating your business.

3. *Education:* No more worthless classes to complain about. Now you can go to school for exactly what you know is most worthwhile to accelerate your career, your earnings. And school doesn't always mean a formal class setting. Read a book. Listen to audiotapes or files. View videos. Find a mentor. Need better closing skills? How about sales management and coaching help? Would you like to be better at Guerrilla Marketing and do lead generation like never before? Go back to school. Here's one warning (and a sad comment on many companies' attitudes toward education): If your firm won't pay for you to "go to class," you have to ask yourself what kind of return you'd get from getting better. Don't be discouraged if your company won't pay for training or support products. I'm shocked at the number of companies that refuse to invest in training, despite the overwhelming evidence that it pays off. If you want proof, visit the American Society for Training & Development, ASTD, at

www.astd.org. Either way, NO EXCUSES! You are responsible for your own success and cannot blame your organization for not supporting you. Go invest in education.

Late reggae legend Bob Marley sang a line we can all take to heart, "Everybody wants to go to heaven, but nobody wants to die." This is too true for salespeople. We'd all love rewards without hardship. But it's going to take some improvement, some investment.

Here's an exercise to identify today what you intend to do under each category:

1. *Yourself:* What'll it be? Clothing, image? What needs work?

2. *Your tools:* Don't wait for prices to come down or spend too much time shopping. Pick up the tool now and use it to build your business. List here what needs upgrading or purchasing.

3. *Your education:* Where are you weakest? What associations can help you? Training companies? Books or resources? You'll succeed more quickly in an environment in which you have account-ability with others. So include who will join you on this journey. Maybe it's another person who needs help; perhaps it's just someone to kick you

in the tail and make sure you're putting your learning into play.

Invest now and see what a difference it makes for you and how you're perceived by peers, clients, and yourself!

CHAPTER EIGHT

It's Better to Receive

Mentor Mania and How to Get Some

Crying Over Spilled Ink

It is hot out. It seems even hotter because Scott and his manager are running a half hour late to do a software demo for a large company's corporate headquarters.

The rep and manager swing into the parking lot and grab a close visitor's spot, right in front of the stylish mirrored building.

As the men scramble out of the car, Scott's already agitated sales manager notices that his pen had leaked on his shirt. He loses it right there. Sweating, swearing, and angrily gesturing toward heaven, he whips off his suit coat and quite literally rips off his shirt. Fabric tearing and buttons flying, he wads it up and fires it into the nearby bushes.

Bare-chested, he tears though the trunk. Pulls another shirt from his luggage. Puts it on. Adjusts his tie in the mirrored office window, and into the building they go.

They call at the first-floor reception where the CEO's assistant is waiting to lead them down the hall and into an already filled conference room.

As Scott walks into the room, he looks beyond the waiting board members and there out the window is their car. The sales manager's shirt is stuck in the bushes.

Fifteen people important to their financial futures had had a ringside view of a terrific temper tantrum. There was no happy ending here.

To this day, Scott is very cautious in and around parking areas—no speeding, stealing parking spaces, illegal parking, etc. He considers himself "on" from the moment he drives into the customer's lot.

Postmortem: A manager should mentor a rep, not just in strategies, but also in attitude and behavior. Scott's boss proved he was unworthy to serve as a model for his sales team. Often, others are observing our actions when we least suspect it. Act like a pro, from the moment you get in the car to begin your day until you get home at night. Remember that you're always sending a message to somebody, including yourself.

● ● ●

The next one is not just about a bad, but an evil, mentor. Here Keith's recollection of his manager reveals how rough it would be to work for someone with poor judgment who also blames you for his mistakes!

When You Absolutely Have to Ruin Your Sale Overnight

Keith's boss insisted on tailing along for the sales call of a lifetime. Their company located tax credits for major corporations. The salesman had landed an appointment with a Fortune 100 client who provided package delivery and pickup. You could quickly guess their name.

The sales call went better than expected, and the sales manager and his protégé left, confident that they had earned the company's trust and business. As Keith's boss bragged a bit about the commissions, they planned how to proceed.

"We need to lock them down immediately," Keith was told as they returned to the office. "You prepare the papers and put them on my desk for approval."

The next day, Keith was in early asking the manager if he'd had a chance to go over the contracts. "I did better than that," he replied. "I've already sent them overnight to our new client."

Trouble was, he had overnighted the contracts to the delivery company *using their main competitor*.

Needless to say, a furious company executive refused to sign the contract.

Keith learned two lessons: "Always pay attention to the details. Never again will I let someone else 'take care' of one of my customers."

Postmortem: And you thought sales managers became bosses because they were great salespeople or deserved it. Keith later told me that his manager blamed him for not attending to the details! Keith wasn't around when the package was sent out, so he couldn't be faulted. Regardless of where blame is placed, the lesson is critical for selling professionals. Any little detail can make or break a deal. There's an old proverb that offers a small line—with big implications, ". . . it's the little foxes that spoil the vines." The phrase refers to small creatures that nibble away at the grapes before they can be harvested—sold as food or turned into wine—and generate profits. In essence, you won't get to enjoy the fruits of your labors if you don't watch out for the fine points of doing business professionally. Keith's real lesson? Nobody but Keith is responsible for his success.

● ● ●

In this story a manager's mouth abruptly ends his company's shot at a sale . . .

Attention All Employees: A Sale Is in Progress

While Tim was on a sales call at a large New York–based insurance company, the prospect became very defensive. Tim's team was pitching a $12 million outsourcing program and Tony, the buyer, couldn't seem to pull the trigger and decide whether he would let Tim work with his company.

Tim and his selling partner asked to use a phone to call their headquarters for some directions. The administrator let them into the unoccupied, expensively equipped videoconference room and pointed to a speakerphone. While on the call with headquarters, Tim got quite heated and his language became less than professional and overly loud. He barked out something to the effect of "Screw Tony, like most buyers, he doesn't have a clue." The call finally ended with new marching orders.

As Tim disconnected the phone, a pleasant voice came over the loudspeaker in the room telling them, "Gentlemen, you should know that your entire call had been broadcast over the building's intercom system."

Time froze.

The salesmen were numb.

Dead men walking down the hall.

Tony, the prospect, met them in the hall, unaware of the broadcast as he was in a closed-door meeting during the call. Tim exchanged pleasantries, told Tony that they'd get back with him, and got out of the building as soon as they could.

Needless to say, they didn't get the deal. Tony heard what happened as soon as the reps left. Tim's word to the wise was this: don't trash the prospect while using their phones.

> **Postmortem:** Tim's buyer is clueless, but whose fault is that? Sales skills include helping prospects identify the reasons they need you. But something else happened here. Remember when you were a kid and you had that phrase pounded into your head by parents and teachers alike—"Respect your elders"? Those three words might be better phased, as we attain sales maturity, as "Respect your buyers." Clearly, this manager didn't model this value for his rep. Treat everyone with respect, even when you're ready to walk away from them.

● ● ●

In this tale of selling terror, a rep's boss earns the title of worst mentor on the high seas . . .

Boating Blunder Sinks Deal

Vince, an engineering manager for a consulting firm, described this as his most painful sales experience. His company had been discussing a long-term retainer program with a major boating equipment manufacturer. It appeared that all the pieces were in place. How cool a call is this? The manufacturer's director of engineering invited Vince to spend the afternoon wrapping things up as they cruised Lake Michigan on one of the corporate boats.

Accompanying Vince, however, was his corporate sales manager, who never hid his opinion that engineers can't sell and needed professional salespeople to close deals. The afternoon started off great. The host told Vince that if his group leader signed off on the proposal, it was a go. Mixed in with a discussion of business, the director of engineering, a proper Southern gentleman type, pointed out some beaches that were cleaned up under his organization in his role as volunteer park superintendent.

An hour into the trip, as the craft approached Chicago's Navy Pier, it looked like the sales manager had had too much to drink. That was made clearly evident when he dropped his shorts and exposed his backside to a passing harbor cruise ship. Quietly, Vince tried to tell him to sit down and shut up, but on the small boat, this type of communication was difficult. The manager followed up his performance by "mooning" another ship.

Business talk had dried up by that point, though Vince was very nervous. He wasn't sure if it was because of the sales manager's antics or if they were just finished. The engineer kept his fingers crossed, and nothing else happened until they finally docked.

As they moored the boat, the sales manager finished another bottle of beer, and tossed the empty into the harbor! Remembering the host's efforts on park reclamation, and knowing that there was no way he was going to be able to retrieve that bottle, Vince just hoped it wasn't noticed.

Back in the parking lot, Vince tried to clarify the next step, hoping the sales guy would just keep quiet as he swayed back and forth with his eyes half shut.

It seemed the alcohol-saturated sales manager was done for the day. Until Vince watched in horror as he finished yet another beer and tossed the can into the adjacent park—with trash cans two steps away. Vince retrieved the can and disposed of it properly, but was pretty sure the call was blown.

Confirmation of that came when, after trying to reach the director of engineering for three days, Vince was informed by his secretary that "Our company really wasn't interested in a retainer program—but thanks for your time."

__**Postmortem**__: Vince's response to the titanic-
sized blunder? First thing he did was get out of that
company and start his own firm with people he
respected. The sales gods frowned on that old company as the sales manager's unprofessional behavior sent earnings to the bottom of the charts. The
company filed bankruptcy and is now just a bad
memory. This sunken sales scenario surfaced when
a bad leader appeared and combined a horrible
first impression with a lack of regard for his business sitting on his horizon. That drunken manager
had no respect for his colleague, the prospect, or
his own company. Who would want to work with
or do business with someone who trashes the basic
principles of courtesy? The only thing Vince might
have done to save the sale would be to "acciden-
tally" push his sales manager overboard. For a
healthier sales career, learn to honor those you call
on and work with. You'll find your personal life
rewarded, too.

●　●　●

Another manager, another poor example: In this
story, we can all learn about the value of keeping our
emotions in check . . .

Sales Manager Earns Life Sentence in Voice Mail Jail

Terri and her sales manager had a full day ahead of them: a three-hour drive to deliver a one-hour presentation for their specialty printing services, then the return trip. They began the day anticipating the acquisition of new business.

They were driving to a town that offered an intriguing opportunity. As their sales team was accustomed to calling on the Chicago metropolitan area, the market for what they sold was becoming saturated by big-city competitors. This potential customer was in a small town, which was probably not "hit on" by other firms they competed with. This large manufacturing plant was a user of exactly the type of products their firm sold.

The two of them arrived in town and proceeded to the prospect's office for a 2:00 meeting. They entered the lobby, walked up to the receptionist, and announced their arrival.

The surprised receptionist informed the reps that the contact had taken the day off!

Terri politely told her she would call him tomorrow, and quickly hustled her sales manager out of the lobby before his simmering temper erupted like a volcano. This guy could be very protective of his salespeople's time and had previously vocalized his displeasure in the lobby of a company after being "stood up."

They climbed back into the car, started driving out of the parking lot, and, after a bit of venting, decided the next step would be to call the prospect's office and leave a gentle voice mail. It would be something simple like they'd shown up, missed meeting the man, hoped all was well, and would like to reschedule an appointment. The call was made on the sales manager's cell phone using the speakerphone feature.

After she left the message, both Terri and the sales manager began to rant again. His vicious language revealed his deep resentment toward people who were not civil enough to treat visitors with simple common courtesy. Terri agreed as well, using some not-so-choice language and graphic detail about what she'd like to do to this guy and included what he should go do to himself.

This went on for some 30 seconds, and then they heard a beep.

In that deathly moment of silence the two salespeople realized—half a minute too late—that the entire conversation had been recorded on the prospect's voice mail!

There was absolutely nothing they could do to retrieve their destructive words. After two weeks, Terri called the prospect, acting like nothing happened, to reschedule the appointment.

That was three years ago, and he still won't take her call!

Because of the size of the opportunity, every time a new salesperson starts, the company makes the "rookie" call to try for an appointment. To this day, no one has been successful. Terri is resigned to the fact that they must have to wait until that buyer with the red-hot ears leaves the firm or dies!

Postmortem: Tough scenario for Terri. A malicious message is delivered because her boss didn't have the sense to keep his mouth shut or better yet, express his feelings in a professional manner. So his bad behavior actually dragged his rep deep into anger as well. In this situation, you need to be cool about what happened, then either be a bit forgiving and give the guy another chance or just let it go—walk away from it. Team selling is good. Team griping is not. Rage has no place in our profession. Learn to manage your feelings as you generate emotions in prospects to help them buy. But save your emotions and express them when you feel genuine joy with new customers and family and friends.

●　●　●

What can you learn from how a business professional handles his shortcomings? In this story, it's another lesson in what not to do . . .

How to Keep Your CEO from Passing Out on Sales Calls

Craig is president of a security firm. Working in teams of detectives, they are hired by other companies to monitor workers' compensation fraud, employee theft, and a variety of what you might call hidden sins inside a firm—sort of corporate narcs. The actual work can range from boring to fascinating. Some staff are assigned to jobs inside companies—to spy on fellow employees. Other detectives do surveillance detail—to find out if "injured" workers are really laid up for workers' compensations claims or whether they're on top of the world, say, roofing their homes.

Occasionally, the firm has struggled when Craig, who is diabetic, doesn't regularly check on his blood sugar until it's too late. In this case, they had landed a sales appointment at a paper company that was losing product to employee theft. A $96,000 investigation contract was on the line. During the big meeting, Craig's condition was beginning to show as he was starting to fade. Usually, when Craig's blood sugar begins bottoming out, his staff insists that he eat something. (They find this preferable to him taking out a hypodermic syringe and shooting up in front of potential clients.)

So it happened that the prospect's general manager was talking when Craig began sneaking bites of a sandwich he'd hidden beneath the boardroom table. The sales team hoped that the guy wouldn't notice, but the prospect stopped talking, grinned, and asked, "Craig, do you have enough for all of us?"

It was embarrassing. In a previous client meeting, Craig had once seemed drunk, when what he really needed was his medicine. He was doing the talking and began rambling, switching the subject from business to baseball. Another time, his condition hit him while he was tailing a suspect during a mobile surveillance job. A colleague had to "run him off the road" in his own car to keep him from killing anyone. You can imagine that killing a client or surveillance suspect would be very bad for business.

The guy at the paper company was gracious when Craig meekly explained what was happening. But the detectives didn't get his business. You can't really blame the prospect. You'd be a little nervous signing a contract with a vendor who has a problem like that—you know, wondering if he'd always be able to perform for a company laying out about $100,000.

It was the final straw: From now on, Craig would take care of his condition before meetings, or excuse himself—without explanation—during them.

   Postmortem: Egos are like big termites that eat away at the structure of a business relationship. They might be the #1 factor in the collapse of business deals. Here, the president didn't want to reveal his physical problems, so he chose to ignore them—at the cost of losing a potential client. When any problem recurs, decide ahead of time how to manage it. This prevents unnecessary surprises during sales calls. Great leaders deal with their shortcomings. They lead by showing their team how to get beyond conditions, physical or mental, that hold them back. Great mentors figure out solutions that work around or through their limitations. Simply put, don't let your ego keep you from asking for help when you need it most.

● ● ●

Okay, we're finally arriving at learning what to do from others. Here, a good mentor uses humor and creativity to turn a dumb mistake into a memorable day of selling.

Flat Sales

Gary is a poor rep for Pitney Bowes. He's poor because he is new at selling and today it really shows.

Gary can't afford a classy briefcase so he bought one of those really cheap vinyl ones. This is what really cheap looks like: The wood frame was balsa wood—the stuff kite frames are constructed with.

It was one of those days when you have to travel with your sales manager. (Note: When that happens, your manager either doesn't trust you or he's training you or he's in your car, hiding from his boss.)

So Gary was poor and cheaply outfitted and nervous as well.

The two men were getting ready to go out on calls, and Gary was rearranging all the junk in the back of his car. He removed a smelly gym bag, that briefcase, and company brochures and reloaded it all into a somewhat organized pile.

As the rep pulls from the curb a small thump and crunch stop him. He looks at his manager, whose eyebrows are raised in interest.

Gary bolts around the back of the car and picks up what was formerly a flimsy briefcase. It is now a splintered mess. Cheap wood sticks out of cheap, shredded vinyl, and it's flat—like one of those cartoon characters after a steamroller crushes the character.

"I can't believe this!" Gary cries, and dives back into the car with the ex-briefcase.

The manager grins and says, "Don't throw it out! We can use it. You're taking this into every prospect's office today. Everyone will feel sorry for your poor appearance. IT'S THE SYMPATHY CLOSE!"

So now Gary was poor and cheap and nervous and stupid.

But the day took a turn in the right direction. The two men they met had a great laugh over Gary's misfortune. The dead case served its purpose—it gained them rapport and a shot at future business. Who would think that a dumb blunder could pay off so well?

    Postmortem: Gary, there's a great lesson here. The wisdom of your manager should inspire every sales pro out there to find a mentor. Look for someone who has been there, been beat up, and become successful in sales. Ask them to advise you. The mentor will be flattered, and you'll be enriched by his or her wisdom and experience. We need experienced experts in our lives. Here's the reasoning behind why that matters to you . . .

There's an old vaudeville skit where a man comes crying to his physician:

"Doctor, I don't know what's wrong with me, but I hurt all over. If I touch my shoulder here, it hurts; and if I touch my leg here, it hurts; and if I touch my head here, it hurts; and if I touch my foot here, it hurts."

"I believe you've broken your finger."

We need doctors for the same reason we need sales coaches and business mentors—because their vast experience gives them the ability to diagnose trouble, then offer a solution or healing remedy. We are too often clueless as to the root cause of our shortcomings because we are too close to the situation to clearly see that trouble. And we are too close to find the path away from it.

Here is how you can center on your mentor. To find the perfect match to push you into a world-class level of selling, ask yourself, ask your colleagues, who would be a dream coach and counselor. Humbly call and request a few minutes of that person's time. Explain your passion for your common interests and ask if he or she would be open to filling the role of an advisor, guide, or guru. Limit your time to what he or she can share or spare, unless it's a paid relationship (that's fine, too), where you'll have scheduled appointments.

Be prepared with some specific goals you can share that can help your mentor form a vision for how he or she can support and teach you. Most great businesspeople are great vision casters, so this is key to showing that you are a serious student. Don't forget to pick your mentor's brain beyond specific advice, with questions like this:

- What books most influenced him or her?

- What magazines does he or she read now?

- What associations are worth joining or ignoring?

Make sure that you take action on your mentor's suggestions and provide feedback as to the impact of that wisdom—on yourself and your marketplace. From the mentor's perspective you then become part of his or her success story as you follow his or her lead and reinforce the value he or she contributes to that world, that industry, and you, the student.

Say thank-you often and in diverse ways. Send notes and gifts. Offer to serve the mentor in some fashion. Volunteer where your mentor does. You might be surprised at how helping your coach can further accelerate your education.

It's Better to Receive • Wrap-Up

I encourage you right now to list three potential and potent mentors. Send a letter or call them to initiate the relationship. You can accelerate your career when you center on your mentor.

Find a mentor today—you will pay yourself handsomely tomorrow.

CHAPTER NINE

Final Thoughts: The Purpose of Our Profession

What Are We Selling For?

What are we selling for? For that matter, what are we here on this planet for? Could the two be tied together?

A few years ago, my family was on vacation visiting the in-laws in St. Louis and Josh, my seven-year-old, ran crying into the house. His face was covered with wood chips and a bizarre lump, a knot sticking out below his right eye. It was gruesome. He was making all these kid crying noises, which meant without an interpreter we had no clue what happened.

Rebekah, our youngest, came in to translate. "Josh climbed a tree and fell out. He climbed a tree higher than the top of the house."

"Show me the tree." And I was led to the backyard where she pointed to a tree towering above the roof.

"Josh fell and landed on his head. His hands were at his sides and he just flew straight down and landed on his head."

How could this boy be standing in the living room crying on my wife's shoulder?

Now I was scared, so we drove to the hospital.

The doctor tested Josh's neck, shoulders, spine—all the things that should have broken from this fall. And every 15 seconds or so she glanced up at me with this funny look on her face.

"He fell how far?" About 18 to 20 feet.

"Landed on his head?" Right, that's the lump (now disappearing) below his eye.

"Let's get his head X-rayed."

Our doctor was baffled by Josh's lack of serious injury. The X-ray of his skull was 100 percent normal, and they gave Josh his own big black photograph of that invincible head. It sits above his bed today.

As my wife Wendy and I sat at his side, I began fighting tears, "He should be dead or at least have a broken neck." She began to tear up as well, shaking her head, not wanting to think those thoughts.

We drove back to her parents' home and all we could talk about was this . . .

Why was he still here? Why was Josh still alive?

So here's the big takeaway, a question.

What are you here for?

Have you had your tree experience? Days after Josh fell from that tree I shared the story with a bunch of ballplayers I work out with. Many started remembering their own moments—accidents on the road, in the house, rough childbirths, you can imagine how many ways someone can suddenly, unexpectedly exit this planet.

Now you might think that those stories aren't about selling. But they are all about selling.

Your life is meant to touch others. We are all meant to connect and contribute to the earthly experience of people we work with, live with, sell to.

See, I used to think selling was about the battle with the bad guys and the celebration of the good guys. Now I treasure both characters.

The depth of your existence is related to your interactions with everyone. Are you aware of the wild variety of people that exist within your circle of influence? Different looks, voices, shapes, clothes; preferences for food, cars, and hobbies. Are you willing to learn from each one—again, some showing you what to do, others teaching you what not to?

We talk about; we are all about gathering wealth. That takes a long time. Be grateful for the time and the people you are given. That's the real reason you're here.

In our family we have a mission statement. It's vague enough to apply to anything, but specific enough that you know when it's happening. We all use it, six-year-old twin girls, eight-year-old son, my wife, and I.

Our mission statement is *BE A BLESSING.*

I trust that through these stories and their lessons I have managed to be a blessing to you.

I hope that you will go back to your sales world and better your owners and managers, your coworkers, and especially your prospects. So go, and . . .

BE A BLESSING.

Appendix

Appendix A

WHERE DO WE GO FROM HERE?

In this *Sales Autopsy* book you learned some lessons that were new and you were reminded of those you already knew. The question you want to ask yourself here is what are you going to do about it all?

As a trainer who speaks, I'm often frustrated that I can't see improvement from my audiences, most of whom I never again encounter. A "before" and "after" in quality of skills and results proves that I've succeeded. But that's the nature of keynote speaking as opposed to training.

You, however, have invested time and brainpower in a unique and useful book. Think about doing more than being entertained by some fun stories and good lessons. Think about improving your sales existence right now.

Remember that change formula?

$$C = D \times V \times F > S$$

You'll improve (Change) when you combine **Dis**-satisfaction (what do you need work on) with a **Vision** for the future (cast by the concepts in this book) with **First Steps** (answer the three questions below) when all these are greater than your **Status Quo** (current state of performance).

1. What did you find interesting, fun, useful?

Sometimes it is just fun to learn something. We also want to learn what can be applied to improve ourselves. List both here.

FUN

USEFUL

2. What did you learn about yourself?

To paraphrase Socrates, "A wise man knows what he doesn't know." A modern version of this wisdom comes from Clint Eastwood in his Dirty Harry movie role *(Magnum Force)*, "A man's gotta know his limitations." Some information affirms we're already doing things right. Other advice points to problems that need correction. List here what you learned related to your experience and what you need to grow.

3. Who will you teach this to?

The best learners teach others immediately after acquiring new knowledge. They realize that by helping those others, a teacher becomes an expert quickly. List here the people you know that would love to hear some ideas, even some you felt were useful from this book. After their names, list what you want to share with them.

1.

2.

3.

4.

5.

Congratulations, you're on your way. And you've not only helped yourself, you've added to the quality and ability of other salespeople with whom you shared these ideas.

Appendix B

Revenge of the Reps: The Video Game

You can't take it anymore. I can't either.

You are sick of beastly buyers and pathetic prospects who hide behind voice mail, lie to you, and generally make your sales life unbearable.

Even rejoicing in the misfortunes of other sales blunder victims in this book can't get you past these professional parasites.

Would you feel better if I gave you a gift?

I have a prescription that can get you fit for work again. Fill it and be healed at *www.RevengeoftheReps.com.*

When you arrive there you will receive the tools to get revenge on these evil scoundrels. As you watch the streets in your territory fill up with prospects, notice how they toss nasty objections at you . . .

"I won't buy from you or your descendants."

"If you'd lower your price to match your IQ . . ."

"I would like to see you—on a milk carton."

"You sales vampires are sucking the blood out of buyers."

"I was frightened by a salesman at birth."

"You remind me too much of my mother."

"I need references; this time no relatives!"

"I need to talk to my spouse, partner, accountant, spirit guides."

"I hate salesmen; my ex-husband is one."

That's enough!

Pick up your giant mutant laser pointer and begin blasting away.

All the pressure you felt butting heads with buyers during cold calling and telemarketing will dissipate as these characters dramatically disappear from the screen.

This free, Xbox-quality graphic game was made just for you, compliments of me, your author.

No more lead-generation nightmares, just justice and revenge at *www.RevengeoftheReps.com.*

Appendix C

Things You'd Love to Say to Evil Prospects: An Exercise

Do you want to have one of the most enjoyable sales meetings your company has ever experienced?

Do this exercise: Have everyone list the eight or ten most frequent (or most exasperating) objections you encounter.

Split up into small groups, and assign a couple of objections to each.

Reality is that we gripe and grouse about these prospects' critical comments anyway. So today each team lists every sarcastic comment or rebellious remark they could think of.

This is like open season and you get to take a verbal shot back at each buyer.

Like any brainstorming session, just record anything that is contributed.

Have the whole team come back and start sharing your vindictive and inflammatory responses.

Create more as you go along. Others will piggyback on your ideas.

Congratulations, you've now developed a supplement to your training manual.

This newly designed document makes a great statement about your culture at work. Everyone wants to have fun while making money; you have just affirmed, in print, that you do that here.

Here are some samples to get your juices flowing . . .

"Wanna think it over . . ."

Maybe you should go home and ask your parents. You might even get your laundry done.

"Send literature"

Would you accept an inordinately large COD package?

"I'll get back to you"

You lie so easily, have you ever considered sales?

"Cheaper somewhere else"

Jeez, you are something. You probably recycle your own toilet paper.

"I need to speak with my boss/partner/invisible man"

You couldn't fill up your fist with Milk-Bones and communicate a command to a dog. Just put me through to him.

"Under contract"

For an additional $300 our attorney can break your existing contract and put you into an ironclad one with us.

"Cost too much"

Many of our clients identify the department most affected by this product and borrow money from its employees—you can even do direct withdrawal from their paychecks.

"Tried before, didn't work out"

Lotta people only try things once. You probably only have one child, eh? It didn't work out? Right—we don't work with quitters anyway.

"Not interested"

You were interested enough to talk with me just now. How much of a bribe do you normally require?

"Price too high"

I could tell by the quality of your clothes. Perhaps a relationship with us would create the momentum to upgrade several areas of your life. Certainly you're spouse would agree—if he or she is still with you.

There you are. Do all meetings have to be somber and boring? Consider this a miniretreat. One hour of mayhem and fun. Start your day with some serious laughter.

Oh, don't forget to send me a copy of what you create. This is too much fun to keep to yourself: dan@salesautopsy.com.

Appendix D

Your Most Embarrassing Moment Selling

Want to appear in my next book?

What is the stupidest, most horrible thing you've ever done on a sales call or in your selling-related work?

Anonymity guaranteed.

Everyone whose story is used will receive a copy of *The Sales Comic Book*—there is nothing like it on this planet (possibly any planet)!

Send me an e-mail at *warstory@salesautopsy.com* and share your most embarrassing moment selling. Don't forget to tell me your lesson learned.